CONFESSIONS OF A JEWISH PRIEST

CONFESSIONS OF A JEWISH PRIEST

From Secular Jewish War Refugee to Physicist and Episcopal Clergyman

Gabriel Weinreich

The Pilgrim Press
Cleveland

to MAX WEINREICH

who taught me the meaning of integrity
this book is dedicated by a grateful son

The Pilgrim Press, 700 Prospect Avenue, Cleveland, Ohio 44115–1100
thepilgrimpress.com

© 2005 by Gabriel Weinreich

The cover photographs, from the author's family album, show (clockwise from left): The author, Dr. Gabriel Weinreich; his mother, Regina, and her younger brother, Yasha, in the Weinreichs' Vilna apartment, 1936; and Gabi, his father, Max, at the typewriter, and his older brother, Uriel, around 1932.

Printed in the United States of America on acid-free paper

09   08   07   06   05   5   4   3   2   1

Library of Congress Cataloging–in–Publication Data

Weinreich, Gabriel.
    Confessions of a Jewish Priest : from secular Jewish war refugee to physicist and Episcopal clergyman / Gabriel Weinreich.
        p. cm.
    Includes index.
    ISBN 0–8298–1695–X (cloth : alk. paper)
    1. Weinreich, Gabriel.   2. Christian converts from Judaism—Biography.   3. Episcopal Church—Clergy—Biography.   I. Title.
BV2623.W45A3 2005
248.2'46'092—dc22

2005049297

CONTENTS

Contents ⁊ *vi*

PART TWO

The Seeing of My Eye

Acknowledgments

Numerous colleagues have read and commented on the manuscript as it developed; in particular Jonah Kalb, my old friend from George Washington High School in New York City in the early 1940s, providentially surfaced after many decades just in time to supply me with much invaluable guidance and encouragement. I am grateful also to Ulrike Guthrie, my editor at The Pilgrim Press, whose many suggestions have improved the book immeasurably. Not least, there would have been no book without the patience, love, and encouragement of my dear wife, Gerane.

My Bible quotations generally follow the Revised Standard Version except for occasional translational modifications of my own; I also quote verbatim from the Episcopal Book of Common Prayer, in both its 1928 and 1979 versions. All those quotations are identified in a short citation index at the end of the book. Excerpts from my father's letters were translated by me from the original Yiddish as published by Avrom Sutskever in *DI GOLDENE KEYT,* Periodical for Literature and Social Problems, Published Quarterly by the General Federation of Labour in Israel, Tel–Aviv, Nos. 95–96, 1978.

Finally, I give thanks to Almighty God for granting me the time and energy to see this book, so important to me, through to publication.

Ann Arbor, Michigan

When I was a little boy, I once asked my father the difference between the beliefs of Christians and of Jews, and he replied: "Jews believe that the Messiah will come at some time in the future, whereas Christians believe that he has already arrived." Since I associated the coming of the Messiah with an abrogation of the need ever to eat spinach again, not to speak of the disappearance of terrible things like wars and poverty, it appeared to me from what my father said that Christians must be very, very naïve people— or else that I hadn't properly grasped his explanation. I did, however, understand that the comparison he had been making was between *religious* Christians and *religious* Jews. This meant that "we"—a pronoun that in my mind included not only our family but essentially all the people with whom our family ever came into contact—were excluded from the comparison because "we" were not religious; specifically, "we" regarded the Messiah as a purely fictitious being.

That is why today, when people ask me to tell them "about my conversion," I generally find myself at a loss. A radical conversion did indeed take place in my life beginning about thirty years ago, but it was not from Judaism to Christianity (which is what most questioners have in mind). Rather, it was from being not religious to being religious, that is, from thinking that the universe can be understood purely rationally to thinking that this is not so. By embracing the first of those beliefs I did not, of course, mean that rational discourse has all the important answers already available but that the methods of investigation that it encompasses, which include scientific inquiry, can ultimately be applied to the solution of all important questions. Today I don't think so.

Yet the result of this conversion did take on a rather specific form. Today I am not merely religious but a Christian, and not merely a Christian but an Episcopalian; in fact, I am an ordained priest within the Episcopal Church. This means a great deal more than doubting the universal efficacy of reason in addressing human questions; among other things, in my particular case it means regularly attending Saint Clare's Episcopal Church in Ann Arbor and engaging in the various weird activities that Episcopalians do in church. (Being a priest, I actually used to lead a congregation in those activities until my retirement, and still do it from time to time.) Why, I am occasionally asked, if I used to be a nonreligious Jew and then decided to become religious, did I not choose the "logical" next step and become a rabbi? To me neither choice, the rabbinate or the priesthood, seemed particularly logical. The fact that I was a Jew was, indeed, supremely important to me, more important perhaps than life; but my Jewishness—of this I am profoundly convinced—in no way departed from me when I acquired a clerical collar. To explain this fact, so paradoxical to many people, is the first purpose of this book.

That purpose, however—the part that narrates my journey from a Yiddish-speaking middle-class Jewish boy in prewar Poland to an elderly Episcopal priest and professor of physics in contemporary Ann Arbor—occupies only the first half of the book. The remainder is an account of my (partly concurrent) journey to faith, that is, my metamorphosis from a person who believes that every subject in the universe can be understood by pure reason to thinking that this is not so. Since this area is, by definition, closed to strictly rational discourse, it makes for a writing paradox even greater than the first.

"I had heard of you by the hearing of the ear, but now my eye has seen you" is Job's final acknowledgment of God's overpowering grandeur, in effect affirming that even forty chapters of the most sublime poetry cannot adequately describe the understanding that comes from a direct face-to-face encounter with the divinity. That's why I have named the first part of this book "The Hearing of My Ear"; it represents the section that fits easily into verbal narration. The second part, entitled "The Seeing of My Eye," tries to guide the reader alongside me through the spiritual transformation that the last few decades have brought.

This book is not meant to convince, let alone "convert," anyone, since I have never felt that the path I chose is necessarily the right one for anyone else. In fact, I deeply believe that there are as many "right paths" as there are people in the world—if not, indeed, many more. But if this theological autobiography leads readers to an empathetic understanding of my life as it has unfolded, and especially if aspects of their own lives become clarified as a result, then my purpose in writing it will have been amply fulfilled.

PART ONE
The Hearing of My Ear

1 ✂ ORDINATION

One winter day when I was not quite eight years old,
attending second grade in one of the secular Yiddish-
speaking elementary schools in my home city of
Vilna, I once noticed a group of classmates excitedly
giggling over some new game at recess; and as I approached they
called out "Let's try it out on Gabi!" They then asked me whether
I could spread the fingers of both my hands two by two, like two
boldface "V for victory" signs, and when it turned out that I could
they gleefully cried, "Gabi is a *kohen*! Gabi is a *kohen*!"

When I went home that afternoon I found my father working
at his rolltop desk in the great big bookshelf-lined room that
served as his study. My father was research director (as well as one
of the founders) of YIVO, an academic research and education institute devoted to contemporary Jewish history and other areas of
social science concerning Jews. Although he had a comfortable of-

1

fice in the YIVO building he often worked at home to avoid being distracted by administrative matters. I stood quietly at the door and, when he looked up, I asked: "Papa, what's a *kohen?"* "A *kohen,* my child," he replied, "is a priest. The *kohanim* were the people who officiated when the Temple still stood in Jerusalem." I then asked, "Why did the kids call me a *kohen* because I was able to spread my fingers?" and he smiled. "There are some Jewish families," he explained, "that carry as part of their family tradition the knowledge of being descended from the hereditary Temple priesthood; and on some special occasions during the year the men of those families, if they are religious, are called to the front of the synagogue to give the people their priestly blessing, using that ancient gesture of spreading the fingers of both hands by twos. Of course the idea that one can recognize a *kohen* from the fact that he is able to spread his fingers in that manner is just an old superstition; but, as a matter of fact, our family *is* one that carries that pedigree, and so you are, indeed, a priest."

Exactly fifty years later—on January 18, 1986—I was ordained a priest at the Episcopal Church of Saint Clare of Assisi in Ann Arbor. I was about to turn fifty-eight.

It had been a whirlwind romance: I had only been baptized —that is, officially become a Christian—a little over three years earlier, on All Saints' Day (November 1) of 1982. By contrast, my other profession—that is, my life as a physicist—extended back to when I was eighteen or nineteen, so that my Christianity could be playfully described as an aberration of old age. But the situation was actually a lot more complicated, as it always is, which is why I chose to begin my narrative with this particular elementary-school incident, illustrating as it does both the continuity of my life and one of its great zigzags.

I was born on February 12, 1928, in a city of northeastern Poland called Vilna, with a population of about 200,000 of whom roughly one third were Jews. My mother had been born in the same city thirty years earlier, as had her mother some twenty years before that. Yet they were both born in Russia rather than Poland; and had my children been born in the same city, their birthplace would have been neither Poland nor Russia but

Vilnius, the capital of Lithuania (which it still is today). That's how
unstable political boundaries can be in that part of the world. The
name "Vilna" is traditional in English; in Yiddish, my native language, it is pronounced *vilne*, with the final *e* clearly articulated
like the "e" in "bed."

As a child I knew, of course, that I was a Jew. There was never
any doubt in my mind about that, but neither was there any
doubt that being Jewish has nothing to do with religion. As I understood it, there were indeed Jews who were religious, but that's
because they were poor and uneducated and had not yet freed
themselves of their medieval superstitions. In Vilna, those Jews
lived mostly in an area of slums referred to as "the Ghetto," even
though Vilna had in fact never had a legally constituted ghetto
(that is, a part of town outside of which Jews were by law forbidden to live) until the Hitler invasion of 1941. What imbued my life
with Jewish meaning was the Jewish culture of which I was a part,
whose most obvious feature, in terms of permeating every minute
of every hour of every day, was Yiddish, the language that we
spoke. In this connection it is helpful to know that the word *yidish*
in Yiddish simply means "Jewish." We were Jews and we spoke
Jewish, just as Poles speak Polish, Germans speak German, and
Russians speak Russian.

The path that led from that little boy who was part of the
secular Jewish culture of prewar Poland to an old man who is
both a retired Episcopal priest and a retired physics professor in
Ann Arbor, Michigan, is, of course, long and convoluted, as every
human life is. But if, as I sometimes imagine, God's idea to make
an Episcopal priest out of me took form when I spread my fingers two by two in second grade, I wonder whether God had any
idea what would be involved.

First, there was the matter of Christianity itself. Even as a
small child I knew very well that, other things being equal,
Christians were people to stay away from; and that this was especially true of Christians engaged in doing something religious.
From time to time my friends and I, walking down a wide city
street, would spy (hopefully still some distance away) a procession of men dressed in black with intricately worked white outer

garments, carrying elaborate processional crosses and other in-comprehensible devices. Sometimes a black wagon decorated in gold and drawn by black horses could also be seen. What pre-vented me from observing any more detail was the good sense to duck quickly into a side street and stay out of sight for fear of being beaten up by the swarm of teenagers who always ran alongside such a procession. I knew, perhaps not completely ac-curately, that the people in black with white outer garments were priests, and the thought that I might grow up to be one of them would have turned my stomach.

When I arrived in New York as a refugee in 1941, the element of fear upon encountering a priest quickly evaporated. (For one thing, they didn't walk around in flowing cassocks and wide-brimmed black hats, as they did in Vilna.) Still, I knew that priests were people who dedicated themselves to the practice of religion on a grand scale, which lowered my estimate of their intelligence substantially since it meant believing in supernatural powers and magic, stuff that science had long ago disproved. Somewhere in a book I had read the story of the great French mathematician and astronomer Laplace who, when Napoleon asked him how in the world he could have written his five volumes of *Mécanique céleste* without once mentioning God, replied: "Sire, I have no need for that hypothesis." I might have given the same answer myself.

What did, on the other hand, impress me in America as com-pared to Poland was our lack of segregation. The segregation of Jews that I knew back home was one that we, by and large, em-braced with open arms. We were glad, for example, to have our own schools that functioned in our own language, although we thought it unfair and antisemitic that the Polish government did not subsidize the Yiddish schools as they did the Polish ones. There were, of course, some Jews who advocated assimilation; who indeed felt that there would be less antisemitism if Jews were less insistent on cultivating their own peculiar culture. Nonetheless, even these "assimilationist" Jews did not send their children to the regular Polish schools where they would have to endure all sorts of abuse from the gentile kids and staff. Instead, they created their own private Polish-speaking schools, which differed from the public schools only in having Saturdays rather than Sundays off. (One day off per week was the norm for everybody.) But here in New York I could rub shoulders with all sorts of non-Jewish kids. In fact, a lot of the time I had no idea what their various ethnicities were, since on the one hand the Jews among them did not speak Yiddish, and on the other those whose families were Italian or Greek looked, to my eyes, like they could be Jews as well.

Twelve years after my arrival, in 1953, I got my PhD in physics from Columbia University and started work at Bell Telephone Laboratories in New Jersey. At this point, I felt thoroughly comfortable with non-Jewish friends and acquaintances; I continued to speak Yiddish with my parents and a small number of others, but not with Alisa, my first wife, who didn't know any (although she was Jewish). I was, however, becoming aware at about that time of my enormous interest in what made various people tick—including people who took God, any God, seriously. Indeed, it was soon after starting my work at Bell Labs that Alisa and I gave a Christmas dinner for a group of friends that included a Jesuit priest (he was actually the brother of one of my colleagues), with whom I had a delightful discussion about whether or not the Jewish festival of Hanukkah (which, of course, falls at approximately that same time) is biblical. I said No, he said Yes, until he remembered from his seminary years that the Book of Maccabees, which describes the origin of Hanukkah, belongs to the so-called "deutero-canonical" books, which Catholics include in their Bibles but Jews and Protestants do not. I had never heard that different denominations can differ on what exactly their Bible includes, and I was fascinated. Nonetheless, the question of whether God exists was never opened in the course of that evening.

In 1960, after seven years of doing research at Bell Labs, we moved to Ann Arbor, where I took a faculty position at the University of Michigan "because," I liked to say, "man does not live by research alone" (I would not, however, have known the origin of the quotation I was paraphrasing). Here Dan and Becky were born, and here, in 1970, Alisa died. A little over a year later I married Gerane, who had Cathy, Marc, and Natalie from her first marriage, so that we now had five children between us. Gerane was an Episcopalian, and when I accompanied her to church I found out that the interior architecture of Saint Andrew's Episcopal Church in Ann Arbor was quite beautiful. I also noticed that the hymnals in front of us in the pew had all the hymns notated in four-part harmony. I could read the music fluently, which meant that a few times during every service (to the rest of which I listened only marginally) I had the joy of part-singing along with the rather competent choir, and that was fun. After a while, I began also to pay attention to the section of the service where one of the priests would step up to the pulpit and talk for twenty or thirty minutes. Somewhat to my surprise, I found these sermons to be intelligent, interesting, and often moving, so much so that I frequently approached the preacher after the service to engage him in further conversation. But the idea of ever becoming a priest myself would have continued to strike me as totally weird.

There were a number of important reasons, one might say principles, that mitigated against my even considering it. First of all, I didn't believe in God; second, for me to abandon my Jewishness felt (in spite of my having absolutely no religious background) like the ultimate betrayal of everything my family and I ever stood for; and third, I already had a profession—physics—which, after all, brought me a lot of gratification. Hence, as I began to accompany Gerane to church on Sunday with greater and greater regularity, I was on my guard for any sign that I was about to violate those principles.

It was the second alarm, the one having to do with abandoning my Jewishness for Christianity, that was the first to sound, since it really has nothing to do with becoming a priest but only with the prior step of accepting baptism, which in 1982 I did. I resolved this problem in my own mind by realizing that I was not actually abandoning anything except, perhaps, my atheism; after all, neither Jewish nor Christian law, taken literally, precludes a person from being both a Christian and a Jew at the same time, and that's exactly what I think of myself as being even today. True, on a certain emotional level it still feels like the ultimate betrayal of everything my family and I ever stood for, which witnesses to the power of Judaism as the greatest survival machine the world has ever known; and much as I have tried to free myself of this emotion, I must admit that I would probably not have been able to have myself baptized had my father or mother been alive at the time, thinking how much pain it would have caused them.

For various complicated reasons that we shall talk about later, in the fall of 1982 Gerane and I transferred from Saint Andrew's Church to Saint Clare's, another Episcopal church in Ann Arbor. A few months later our new rector took a three-week vacation and chose three lay parishioners, me among them, to prepare and deliver one sermon each during his absence. So it came about that on May 22, 1983, I stood for the first time before a congregation dressed in cassock and surplice and preached about the meaning of Pentecost. Being something of a ham by nature, I was (in spite of being scared to death) exhilarated beyond belief both by the experience itself and by the rush of compliments that followed, and not long afterwards I began to think seriously about ordination.

It turned out that the policy of the diocese of Michigan at that time was to allow "persons with professional experience, carefully selected, and with educational qualifications" to prepare for ordination in an individual study program approved by the bishop instead of attending seminary. (Traditionally, this option is called "reading for orders"; in the diocese of Michigan it no longer exists.) In view especially of my knowledge of Bible, most of which I had acquired since beginning to attend church, the bishop accepted me into this program, suggesting that if I took a year to study other theological subjects I could then take, and pass, the General Ordination Examination which the National Episcopal Church offers, mostly to seminary seniors. This examination, which occupies a number of successive days, must (according to canon) rigorously cover the following seven subject areas: (1) the Holy Scriptures; (2) Church History; (3) Christian Theology; (4) Christian Ethics and Moral Theology; (5) Contemporary Society; (6) Liturgics and Church Music; and (7) Theory and Practice of Ministry. It is sufficiently difficult so that an appreciable fraction of examinees fail in one or more subjects the first time around, but that did not, thankfully, happen to me; and although I was kept

very busy for the period of my studies, I never did need to inter-
rupt my job as professor of physics. Later, from the time of my ordination in 1986 until my retirement from the two jobs in 1995
and 1996, I was kept busier still by having "two simultaneous full-
time jobs, each of which took up two hundred percent of my
time," as I cheerfully used to describe my situation. This was, of
course, occasionally very hard on my family, particularly on
Gerane; but it did prevent the third of my alarms—"I already have
a job"—from ever going off.

Which left me with only one problem: I didn't believe in God.
True, every time I attended a church service the creed, which begins with the words "I believe in God," was recited, but at first
(when I was merely accompanying Gerane as her guest) I didn't
consider that I needed to join in this since I was only a visitor; as
time went on and in a subtle way I ceased to feel like a visitor, I
would indeed recite the creed but unobtrusively skip the first
word. (Today, I understand that the recitation of the creed is in
any case a *liturgical* act in which the congregation joins in a statement of the historical faith of the Church, rather than necessarily
stating the detailed beliefs of each individual member at that particular moment; so it was really unnecessary for me to go to all
that elaborate trouble and subterfuge.)

Even at my ordination service, the matter did not explicitly
arise. This service, like every service at which the bishop is present, tends to be quite elaborate. The bishop, dressed in his distinctive vestments, is seated in his special bishop's chair before the
packed church and, following the festive processional, the ordinand (in this case, I) stands before him. In the course of a certain
amount of formal questioning, the ordinand signs a declaration
that he believes the Bible to be the Word of God, and solemnly
engages to conform to the doctrine, discipline, and worship of the
Episcopal Church. After this, there are Bible readings, a sermon, the
creed, an outline by the bishop of the duties of a priest after each
item of which the ordinand expresses his assent, and finally the
Consecration of the Priest, in which the ordinand kneels and the
bishop places his hands on his head, at the same time saying the
prayer that includes the clause "Therefore, Father, through Jesus

Christ your Son, give your Holy Spirit to [Gabi]; fill him with grace and power, and make him a priest in your Church." The service then continues with a celebration of Holy Communion.

Taken literally, of course, "the doctrine of the Episcopal Church," to which as part of my ordination I solemnly engaged to conform, includes the content of the creed; but by that time I knew, both from my own experience and from that of my co-parishioners who came to me precisely because they were troubled by this, that items of personal faith cannot be legislated, nor are they ever cast in concrete. I honestly felt I was "conforming to the doctrine of the Church" both by supporting the believers (which I wholeheartedly did) and by helping those who at that moment did not believe but longed to (to which category I found myself, too, belonging). I'm not sure how I would have responded if, in the course of the service, the bishop had asked me directly "Do you believe in God?", but I knew that he wouldn't do that because in a liturgical church the exact text of the ordination service, as well as of every other service, is prescribed in the Book of Common Prayer, and I knew that this question was not there. And so I became a priest.

Earlier in this chapter I suggested, a bit tongue in cheek, that God's idea to guide me through this whole odyssey may have resulted from seeing me spread my fingers two by two in second grade; and I playfully wondered whether God had any idea what exactly was involved. Looking back now, it is impressive how thoughtfully the various steps in this journey appear to have been planned out. After all, if someone (it could not have been God, since I didn't believe in God; it would have to have been some kind of stand-in, like a burning bush) had made the suggestion early in my life that I become a priest, I would have rejected it out of hand. Of course one can argue that this was so because I had no real idea what a priest does, which is undeniable; but if I had been told the truth, namely that a priest is a person who pays an enormous price in effort and time trying (often unsuccessfully) to help others; who constructs and preaches sermons the main point of which his listeners frequently miss; who leads a congregation, or individuals face to face, in prayers for help that often seem to go unheeded; and who (in spite of the incessant frustration and recurrent pain) loves every moment of it, I doubt if it would have attracted me any more. What did attract me powerfully, however, was the beautiful architecture of a church; the opportunity to sing music notated in four parts; and having a captive audience for my preaching. And, at that moment, that was enough.

Today, seventeen years after my ordination, I would say without much hesitation that I *do* believe in God, and that being a priest had a big part in leading me there (rather than *vice versa*). I still appreciate the architecture of a beautiful church, still delight in hymns sung in stirring harmony, still obtain satisfaction from having a captive audience for my sermons and receiving compliments on their form and content. But the truly profound pleasure derives from the frequency with which people who interact with me come away with increased peace of mind and new love for their close ones and for the world generally. It is at times like these that my faith in God is strongest, simply because I know very well that by myself, without a higher power at my shoulder, I simply am not that good.

2 ❁ SIN

Although, as we just saw, belief in God came to me rather late in life, it would be a mistake to conclude that before that I didn't know the meaning of the word "sin." Indeed, if you had asked me—or, for that matter, anyone else—for some illustrations of that concept, you would typically hear examples such as stealing, robbing, committing adultery, wasting food, or refusing to help someone in need. Neither Jews, nor Christians, nor Muslims, nor atheists would have any trouble agreeing with this. But when I once mentioned to a Christian friend that the Jewish religion does not recognize the idea of *original* sin, he asked: Does that mean that in the Jewish Bible the third chapter of Genesis is missing? In case you don't remember, that is the chapter describing how the serpent tempted Eve with the fruit of the tree of knowledge, how (after she had tasted of it) she gave some to Adam also, and how as a result God drove them both out of the Garden of Eden. Quite automatically, a person who grew up in the Christian tradition tends to see in that story the Bible's version of the origin of human depravity: before this "fall of man" took place, Adam and Eve were pure, chaste, and lovable, living happily in their idyllic surroundings; afterwards they, together with their descendants, were unhappy and driven creatures, condemned to eternal misery, possessing a limited capacity for good and an enormous capacity for evil, filling the world with all the pain and suffering that is (alas!) all too familiar to us today. "Sin" is the Christian word for this destructive quality, which is rampant in the world, and "original sin" is the idea that, because of Adam's (and/or Eve's) original act of disobedience, every one of their descendants, even as a newborn infant, is already pseudogenetically endowed with that destructive quality.

It's true that this concept is absent from Jewish theology. In the classical Jewish view, the transgression committed by Adam and Eve was *their* sin, and the punishment of expulsion from the garden was *their* punishment. It did, of course, affect their children and children's children, but parents' behavior always does that. It does not mean that newborn infants come into the world already imbued with sin as an intrinsic quality.

But while I believe that this very quick summary of "official" Christian and Jewish theory on the subject is, as far as it goes, accurate, its actual significance is certainly not self-explanatory. Is it purely a question of abstract theological theory, or does it have any relation to what human beings actually experience?

There are, to my mind, two ways in which original sin manifests itself in human experience. The first is the human capacity to create pain and suffering *without* anybody committing any identifiable transgression. The second, closely related, is people's obsession with their own real or imagined offenses.

Here is a story from my own life that illustrates what I mean.

When I was seven years old, I decided that I would get my father something really nice for a birthday present. For months before, I had walked by the large stationery store on *troker* Street and looked longingly in the window at a gadget for wetting stamps. It was made of solid glass, a tray to be filled with water and a glass cylinder with a glass axle to rotate in two depressions in the side of the tray while dipping into the water. The tray had a further extension with subdivisions for storing stamps of various denominations, and a cover for the whole assembly also molded out of glass. The thing was, I thought, incredibly beautiful; plus, my technical sense was enchanted by the feat of engineering whereby the cylinder, rotating in the pool of water, brought just enough wetness to the top surface to moisten a stamp without getting the user's fingers wet.

The trouble was, I didn't have any money. Unlike my own children years later, who at that age were already getting a small weekly allowance, I had absolutely no sense of what might be a reasonable amount to spend. If I ever needed some money for anything, I went to my father and explained my need; he then, such was my impression, invariably reached into his pocket and gave it to me. Obviously that approach couldn't be used in the present case. But then a miracle occurred. One afternoon, coming home from school and passing through the front hall, I saw a bunch of money lying on the table. I didn't try to count it; clearly there was plenty, and surely nobody could possibly mind if I took a modest amount for the obviously praiseworthy purpose of pleasing my father on his birthday.

I took four one-*gildn* pieces, headed downtown, and breathed a sigh of relief seeing that the object of my desire was still in the window. But then came the big shock: its price, the proprietor told me, was *five gildn!* There was, he said, another one that I could have for only two. It was, indeed, a glass roller in a glass tray, but it was ground rather than polished; what's more, it was just that, a roller and a tray, with no additional space for storing stamps.

Tears had begun to trickle down my cheeks. I confided to the proprietor that it was to have been a gift for my father's birthday, and I had my heart set on the bigger and more beautiful one. He asked how much money I had, and I showed him my four *gildn*. Well, he said after some hesitation, all right. I'll let you have it for four. He even gift-wrapped it for me in magnificent blue paper!

I ran up the long hill home carrying the precious package, full of enormous satisfaction with myself and with the world in general. For the first time in my life, I had done something beautiful on my own, without anyone's help. I was overcome with the sense of that accomplishment, of the wonderful family of which I was a part, of my ability to bring joy to people that I love. And two days later on my father's birthday, when the time for gifts came, I presented him with my beautiful treasure wrapped in blue paper and watched him unwrap it, waiting for the general oohs and aahs.

Suddenly, everything froze into silence.

"Where did it come from?" asked my mother. I explained that I had bought it, and gave the name of the store. "And where did you get the money?" "Oh," I replied, still expecting admiration for my creativity, "I found it lying on the hall table!"

My mother immediately handed me my coat and practically dragged me by my sleeve all the way down to *troker* street, where she stormed into the store, slammed the present down on the counter, and proceeded to berate the proprietor about exploitative people who take money from little boys who can have no understanding of what they are doing. He turned very pale but didn't say a word. When she was done, he stepped over to the cash register, took out a five–*gildn* note, and slapped it down in front of her; he had either forgotten that he had only charged me four, or (this only occurs to me now) his self–respect prevented him from doing anything that might have seemed like haggling. I wanted to say something about the price but I didn't. I hated them both, hated them with a vengeance.

Only some years later did I find out that the cash had been left in the front hall for some tradesman to whom it was owed, who was coming to pick it up. When it turned out to be short, our maid Janina was accused of stealing and given notice. As of my father's birthday she had not yet left, however, so my mother had to go and abjectly apologize, and plead for her to stay. (She did.)

Obviously, that whole sequence of events generated an enormous amount of pain—for me, for the store proprietor, for my mother, for Janina, and of course for my father too. Whose fault was it? Who sinned?

Granted that I am hardly a disinterested observer, I strongly hesitate to place the blame on myself. I was, after all, a very little boy, out to bring my beloved father joy on his birthday. Yes of course, I might have asked my mother for help in obtaining the gift I wanted, but the fact is that within our household there was very little emphasis on the idea of private property, and a lot of emphasis on always sharing. And anyone who understands children will understand the excitement and appeal of doing something like that independently, not by asking mother to do it for me. In principle, the concept of stealing was known to me, and known to be a bad thing, but it never occurred to me that what I had done could, by any stretch of the imagination, be construed to fall into that category.

The store proprietor? Well, yes, he could have asked me not only how much money I had but where I had gotten it, and whether my parents knew about it. One thinks about these things later. At the time, his heart was touched by the little boy intent on pleasing his father, and in despair because he might not be able to do it. He probably had children of his own. To help me out of my crisis, he personally gave up 20 percent of his selling price; in return, he received a venomous dressing-down from an enraged woman who accused him of ugly things. Shall we, then, say that it was his fault?

Or was it my mother? At the very least she might have asked me, when the cash was discovered missing, whether I knew anything about it. ("There was some money left in the front hall which is no longer there. Did you, by any chance, borrow some of it?") After all, to accuse one's maid of stealing is a terrible thing, and might well prevent her from getting another job for a long, long time.

But then again I have to say, before laying the blame on my mother, that I have no idea under what stresses she might at that moment have found herself. A completely unrelated incident comes to my mind that took place five years later, in the summer of 1940, shortly after Vilna returned to Soviet occupation (more about that later). I was twelve, and it was about a year since my father, along with Uriel, had left Vilna to attend an

International Linguistic Congress and been stranded abroad as stateless persons when World War II broke out, leaving my mother and me at home alone. On the evening in question, I had been peacefully walking along the street—perhaps coming home from a friend's house—when I discovered that a most adorable, darling little puppy was following me. I picked it up, petted it, and put it down again on the sidewalk; this time, it remained absolutely glued to my heel. I was touched. I was in love. I took the puppy home to ask my mother whether I might keep it, but Janina (yes, five years later Janina was still with us) told me that my mother was out. She gave the puppy some milk, arranged a little basket for it, and told me to go to bed; when my mother returned, she would ask her about it. I left the puppy crying in its basket and went to sleep.

My mother returned about four in the morning. It seems that two burly men had appeared at the door at suppertime and ordered her to accompany them. They were Soviet secret police. Although their car was taking a circuitous route, my mother, born and raised in Vilna, quickly discerned that they were driving her to the *lukishker* prison, which had a generations-old reputation as a place from which no one returns. Her husband and older son, she thought, were somewhere in a faraway foreign country; her little boy was at home alone. She was taken to a windowless basement room and interrogated continuously for nine hours. They wanted to know where the jewels were that my father had hidden, which belonged to the YIVO but were now the property of the state (needless to say, there had been no such jewels). They said that if she told the truth she could go free; otherwise she would rot.

At half past three in the morning they released her, and she staggered through the iron prison gates into the dark and deserted city. It was about half an hour's walk to our house, up a steep hill, and then three long flights of stairs, before she finally stumbled through the door of our apartment. Janina, terrified, came out to meet her. From the kitchen came the ceaseless whining of the puppy, who apparently hadn't stopped since I went to bed.

"Get rid of that obnoxious animal this instant!" my mother wanted to scream, but only a hoarse rasp came out; she then collapsed on her bed. When I got up the next morning the puppy was gone, and Janina told me that permission for me to keep it had been refused. I could see that my mother was fast asleep, but it didn't keep me from storming into her room and forcibly waking her. "You awful, cruel, unloving woman, you aren't fit to be a mother!" I shouted at her, burst into tears, and ran off. (I did not actually find out about my mother's experiences that night until many years later.)

And so, returning to the episode of my father's birthday present: Whose fault was it? Who had sinned? Alternatively, is it really necessary for someone to have sinned? Or is the question itself perhaps a symptom of our peculiar obsession with "explaining" all suffering as punishment for somebody's sin, often our own?

Which brings us back to the Garden of Eden. According to the first chapter of the Bible, God spent the sixth day of creation forming all the animals, thinking that that would be the end of the task; but as evening approached it felt as though something was still lacking in this marvelously created world. So God said, "Let us make humans in our image," and did. Now there is obviously something very puzzling in this use of the phrase "in our image." Try to enumerate God's most distinctive qualities, and most people will come up with items like *omnipotence*—God can do whatever God wants; *omniscience*—God has complete knowledge of past, present, and future; and *infallibility*—God knows that everything will work out exactly according to the divine plan. Surely we humans are neither omnipotent, nor omniscient, nor infallible! So why "in God's image"?

The answer, I think, is this: we are created in God's image in that we share with God the special combination of free will (being able to decide on our actions) and free judgment (being able to distinguish between right and wrong). This combination (which only God and humans possess) means that we have the terrifying capacity of standing in judgment on our own deeds. It is, of course, also known as having a conscience—which, precisely because of its scary quality, so easily becomes obsessive and cancerous.

I think that this is what the third chapter of Genesis is about: whatever the exact details, it is clear that somebody's memory, or imagined memory, of what happened in the Garden of Eden was immensely frightening. We do know that in the story a tree of the knowledge of good and evil is mentioned, and that Adam and Eve ate of its fruit, and that that's when their troubles began. We know also that in this way conscience, God's great and Godlike blessing, instead remained engraved in the human psyche as God's greatest curse.

So if we ask, as we did at the beginning of the chapter, whether original sin is purely a matter of abstract theological theory or something that relates to what human beings actually experience, the answer is that it is very much part of human experience. It is the compulsion to try to interpret anything bad that happens as somebody's fault and, failing that, to conclude that it must be our own. It is the inability to perceive suffering as anything other than punishment. And in spite of the fact that "original sin" sounds like a technical term of Christian theology (which of course it is), obsession with one's own real or imagined misdeeds is certainly not limited to religious people—let alone to Christians—but seems to be a widespread malaise of our civilization.

What in this context does distinguish a person of faith, such as me, is that (unlike my atheist friends) I am compelled to ask: What is God's response to all of that? No definitive answer to that question is available, but here is how I am personally inclined to imagine it. A few paragraphs ago, I named infallibility as one of God's distinctive characteristics; that is, everything always works out exactly according to the divine plan. But the Bible is full of counter-examples, situations in which God is obviously surprised by the results of what God does—especially when interacting with human beings. I suspect that endowing us with the combination of free will and free judgment was one such case: the resulting prevalence of cancerous consciences was not at all what God had had in mind! If I am right, it would make original sin neither our fault, nor the fault of God, but *a snafu that happened by accident.*

But that does not mean that God is content to leave it that way. In fact, God's concern with how to repair the catastrophe of original sin—or, in the language of classical Christian theology, to bring salvation to humanity—forms, as we shall discover, one of the essential strands in the story of Christianity, and therefore (as we shall see) also of this book.

3 ❧ ANTISEMITISM

Two chapters ago, at the beginning of our narrative, we got a glimpse of little Gabi playing at recess with his second-grade classmates in the obviously peaceful and protected setting provided by our Yiddish-speaking school. As most of us children saw it, the rampant antisemitism in the world around us was a component of reality all right, but not a very pressing one; it almost seemed like the accounts of Jewish persecutions that we got from our classroom study of Yiddish literature, including everything from ancient history up to the major pogroms of 1905, were more compelling.

For us as for the adults, the common Yiddish word for gentiles was *goyim*. Many English speakers are acquainted with that word and are aware that, to a greater or lesser extent, it always carries a derogatory value. From time to time we did have to deal

20

with gentiles for whom a derogatory name was felt to be inappropriate; in that case, the word *krist*, "Christian," was used. So, for example, the apartment facing ours on the third floor of *groyspohulanke* 14 was held by an elderly couple. The husband was, if I remember correctly, a professor at the University of Vilna. I'm not sure I ever knew their name, but whenever they encountered either of my parents on the stairs, the man always raised his hat. (My father could not reciprocate because he never wore a hat, but he did return courteous, if distant, greetings.) To us, they were not *goyim* but *kristn*.

Yet they were the exceptions that tested the rule. Certainly the man's association with Polish academia guaranteed nothing, as Jewish students at the university (those who had somehow made it through the gauntlet of discriminatory exams and regulations) continually experienced. Although still pretty far from university age myself, I clearly remember—because it was talked about widely—how at one point the university legislated that Jews were to be confined to the back benches of lecture rooms. The Jewish students, in protest, insisted on not sitting down at all, knowing, incidentally, that as soon as classes were over they would, likely as not, encounter groups of Polish students in the courtyard assembled for the purpose of beating them up. Those were *goyim*. One didn't refer to them as *kristn* unless one was specifically concerned with their religious persuasion.

I remember once when I was perhaps eight years old, walking along the street at my usual leisurely pace that allowed me to contemplate the world around me while not missing any of my own thoughts, probably (judging by where this incident occurred) on my way home from a visit to my grandmother. It was a balmy late spring day, so I was dressed in a light shirt and short pants, as was customary for boys of my age. Somewhere on *zavalne* Street my attention was caught by a group of three or four young men who were calling out to me. Big and strong and beautiful, they were apparently on break from digging a ditch. Their spades were spread out on the sidewalk as they sat on the curb smoking their cigarettes and happily chewing the fat. When I went over, they asked me how old I was, where I was going, whether I was enjoying the weather, and when school would be out. It was, I felt, a thoroughly pleasant encounter.

The sudden, unexpected and incomprehensible stab of pain made me jump three feet. I regained my balance and turned around wide-eyed, trying to figure out what had happened. The young men were laughing uproariously, elbowing each other and pointing. I then looked down and saw the ugly red spot on my calf where one of them, while chatting with me, had casually ground his cigarette. I turned and ran. There was really no reason to run, since they were not likely to chase me; they had had their fun with the little Jew, and were probably ready to get back to work. Rather, I ran from what had taken place. It's as though I felt that, if I ran fast enough, I could outrun the flow of history and catch up with the time before this horrible event had happened, and so make it not have happened at all.

Yet one may also ask: What exactly was so horrible about it? Not, surely, the burn as such. Playing as we played, climbing trees, falling off fences, slipping on sidewalks, my friends and I incurred a number of injuries every week more serious than that; I know that this must be so because my mother never bothered to ask me what that particular lesion was. No, what was horrible was the betrayal of my trust. They had seemed so nice and pleasant, but in fact they were cruel and mean. They were not *kristn*, but *goyim*; I had ignored that fact, and paid for it dearly.

Of course there were some gentiles with whom I was in frequent contact who were in no way dangerous: our maid Janina; the maid (sometimes there were two) at my grandmother's house; and, of course, the peasants whose farms surrounded my grandmother's place in Niemież, and whom off and on she hired as laborers. However, these were all people who were, in one way or another, indebted to us. When my grandparents bought their summer place in Niemież, the dirt road that led from the cobblestoned highway up to the village was, like everything else around there, pretty solid clay; but one particular stretch went through a depression that collected rainwater, turning it into veritable quicksand. For God knows how many centuries the local peasants had trouble getting their wagons through, needing always to help the horses by removing as much of the load as possible and then having all available men and women lean with all their might to get moving again. The first thing my grandmother did, when she saw the situation, was to have I don't know how many cartloads of sand brought in and dumped in that place at her expense, until the level of the road rose about three feet and the old mired stretch suddenly became comfortably passable. The peasants naturally overflowed with gratitude toward *Pani Doktorowa* (the way a doctor's wife is referred to in polite Polish), and that defined their attitude toward her and her family from then on.

I do have to say, however, that I am not at all sure how the local priest in Niemież felt about members of his flock kowtowing to Jews. Although this fact tends to be overlooked in America today, Christianity is, in its classical theology, a highly antisemitic religion; indeed, the very idea that it is possible to be a good Christian without detesting Jews is probably no more than three hundred years old at the most. I am aware, of course, that throughout history there have been good people who, acting from their hearts, knew that the whole point of God's generous and unmerited love is that we who receive it should allow it to flow out from us in the same indiscriminate way. But as far as official church doctrine is concerned, beginning with the New Testament and continuing through the unanimous teaching of the early church theologians, the Jews, who are seen as having rejected Jesus and brought about his death, have in turn been rejected by God; and the utter destruction of the Jerusalem Temple soon afterwards, as well as the dispersion of the nation of Israel far and wide from its homeland, are taken as incontrovertible proofs of this. That is certainly the way in which the four Gospels present the matter.

Now it is not difficult to see how Christianity, having once gotten started with that version of the story, would find it strengthened more and more as the centuries rolled on. To begin with, the Gospels do present what is, on its own terms, a highly compelling plot. Even though Jesus spends most of his earthly ministry healing, preaching salvation, and generally doing good among his own people (that is, among Jews), he ends up betrayed and abandoned by them when things turn ugly. "His blood be on us and on our children!" shouts the Jewish mob when Pilate expresses qualms about putting Jesus to death. Even the name of his arch-betrayer, Judas, sounds (in all languages) like "Jew." From that point, it is not hard to fast-forward any number of centuries and find the Jews still there, miserable, persecuted, and abused. "His blood be on us and on our children," they had said; now God is giving them what they deserved and asked for.

Yet the curious thing is that while it is easy to understand how, once begun, such a story would propagate and grow, we know essentially nothing about how it originally started. Not only do all our documents come from a time after the break between Christians and Jews had already taken place, but they are themselves *Christian* documents designed to proclaim the young Christian faith, including the part about the purported role of the Jews in the crucifixion. Clearly, to search such sources for the origin of the beliefs that they proclaim would be begging the question. What we can say, however, is that based on such factual history as we do have, the story related by the Gospels in this regard lacks all plausibility. The general teachings of Jesus of Nazareth, as they are repeated there, are actually rather closely related to what we independently know of the Pharisees; and while both would have had their opponents, it's very unlikely that such opposition would reach the level of murder, judicial or otherwise. By contrast, the sight of a charismatic preacher entering Jerusalem just days before the great festival of Passover (when the influx of pilgrims was already providing plenty of potential mob material) would certainly alarm the Roman authorities. Under those circumstances, their decision that prudent crowd control dictated getting that troublemaker out of the way is so utterly plausible that it almost qualifies as a no-brainer.

To a Christian person of faith like myself, the situation presents a serious problem. It's not the factual inaccuracy of the biblical narrative that troubles me: although I know that some people feel otherwise, I myself do not regard the Gospels as books of history, any more than I regard Genesis as a book of history. To me, the Bible is the Word of God, and to take it as a mere recitation of facts, like a telephone book, is (to my mind) simply not taking it seriously enough. The Genesis account of creation is God talking to us, and it is for us to ponder the meaning, which, in our perception, may even be continually changing; but if geologists tell me that, in fact, the world was not formed in the span of six days, I don't find it the least bit disturbing. In the same way, I am not troubled to think that the Gospel story may not be factually correct; it does not in the least interfere with my search for God's meaning that is contained in it.

No; the problem I perceive is that, *as a result of* the Gospel story, the Jews have in the course of the succeeding two thousand years gotten an incredibly raw deal, of which the Holocaust of the middle of the twentieth century was the most horrible, but by no means the unique, representation. Faced with such a reality, a person of faith cannot but cry out: why did God do that? How could God do that? Sure, the Gospels as we have them make a good story, but did God lack the imagination to invent another story that would accomplish equally well what needed to be accomplished without resulting in two millennia soaked in Jewish blood?

It is not, alas, given to us to look into the mind of God, but perhaps I can share with the reader two thoughts that I have, at various times, had on the subject. Neither one provides a full and satisfactory explanation of this great theological conundrum; nonetheless, I have at times felt truth in both of them.

The first is that when God originally formed the Jews as a "stiff-necked people," he may himself have underestimated the survival power with which that quality endowed them. After all, the Bible mentions many nations—such as the Canaanites, the Hittites, the Amorites, the Perizzites, the Hivites, the Jebusites, whose lands were promised by God to Moses at the burning bush; the Midianites, whom Gideon fought; the Philistines, who were the enemies of Samson and later of David; the Assyrians, who destroyed the kingdom of Israel; the Babylonians, who sacked the Jerusalem Temple and drove the remaining Jews into exile; and later, of course, the great world empires of Greece and of Rome, who occupied and colonized the territory of Palestine, destroying the Second Temple in the year 70 C.E. and finally, after one Jewish revolt too many, leveled Jerusalem in 135. Yet every one of those empires disappeared soon afterwards like the snows of yesteryear, whereas the Jews remained.

Perhaps God had had in mind that, to later readers of the Gospels, Jews—like Pharisees, Sadducees, Herodians, and for that matter dragons and unicorns—would be fairy tale characters, mythical beasts; and that Christian manifestations such as medieval Passion plays (still produced in some places in Germany), which often represented Jews as having horns, could not inspire their audiences to go out and burn down the ghetto for the simple reason that no real live contemporary Jews would any longer exist. But here God was outwitted by the stiff-necked group of rabbis who convened at Jamnia (a small town thirty miles northwest of Jerusalem) after the fall of the Second Temple and in effect invented what we today call *rabbinic Judaism*, independent of Temple or territory, built instead on an incredibly concentrated, incredibly inward-looking, and incredibly stubborn way of life that turned out to be the most highly perfected survival machine the world has ever seen. That might be one possible explanation.

The other is hazier and more complex, and concerns the nature and purpose of suffering itself. To a Christian especially, the agony of Christ on the cross is, after all, a most central event of cosmic history, and in that case the question "Why did God do it?" has been asked since the beginning; but the most frequently given answer, that it has something to do with atonement for our sins, has to me never seemed satisfactory (more on this in later chapters). Yet even if we don't know the answer to the question, there are some things we learn from the fact itself: in particular, it tells us that since it was Christ, whom Christians believe to be divine, who experienced that agony, *suffering must itself be an attribute that is shared by God.* Looked at in that way, Jewish tribulation through the centuries may take on a rather different shading. Granted that no clear and obvious explanation comes out of this, at the very least it helps us to see how, far from representing God's rejection, Jewish history may on the contrary somehow signify his special trust and love. In fact, I cannot help feeling that the Jewish community in which I grew up, although it was not religious and did not believe in God, must have had some unconscious perception of that special trust and love, which gave us the strength to resist the antisemitic hooliganism around us while continuing our otherwise normal existence.

But when my family settled in the United States in 1941, it was with the understanding that, in this country, antisemitism does not exist. That's part of democracy; that's part of freedom; at least that's how I, at the age of thirteen, understood it. There were, to be sure, rumors of country clubs and college fraternities that would not accept Jews as members, but this always struck me as a silly concern. Back home, my friends and I attended Yiddish schools, patronized Jewish stores (where Yiddish would be the normal language of communication), and generally lived as part of a proud community for whom "acceptance by gentiles" was a nonissue: who would want to mix with them anyway? In the same way, I asked myself, who in the world would want to belong to a non-Jewish college fraternity or country club? The important thing is that the *active* form of antisemitism, the kind that was ready at any moment to take the initiative in inflicting physical violence on me, no longer needed to be worried about.

This point of view was, however, tested by an experience I had a year or two after our arrival. Payson Avenue, the street on which we lived in upper Manhattan, runs alongside Inwood Park, a beautiful semiwild tract that extends to the Hudson River, where I would often take walks by myself, admiring the outcroppings of rock that are so characteristic of Manhattan Island. Occasionally, too, I would bring a book and sit down on a bench to read, as I did one afternoon when I was enjoying a new novel: *di mishpokhe karnovski (The Family Karnovski)* by I. J. Singer. It was a pleasant day, and I expected no disturbance, when I was suddenly accosted by a girl and two boys a couple of years older than I, who were clearly up to no good. My trying to ignore them (as I had always been taught to do) didn't work, and since they were now on all sides of me there was also no place to retreat. "Look at him!" jeered the girl, "I wonder what he's reading?" With this she snatched the book out of my hands, looked mockingly at the Yiddish text, then threw it into a nearby trash can full of paper that someone had earlier set on fire.

I sat transfixed, immobile, surely with no trace of blood in my complexion, until they had had enough and romped off to their next adventure, when I leaped up and with the help of a few sticks rescued my smoldering book and examined what was left. It was a big fat novel, so of course most of the pages had the printing still intact, but the covers were gone and everything else was pretty dramatically charred around the edges. In this state I carried it home and, having made sure that the fire was safely out, buried it in a drawer of my chest.

There were a lot of reasons why I didn't tell a soul: feelings of shame, misgivings about my own guilt, and of course the overwhelming sense that if one refuses to talk or think about it then it won't have happened. Then there was the suspicion (not surprising in an adolescent boy) that, had I been more masculine, more of a *man*, I could have taken charge of that woman by sheer male authority. And that's where the matter might have rested had I not, two weeks later, run into one of the two boys of that trio at the Dyckman Street subway entrance. To my enormous surprise, he greeted me in a friendly fashion and asked: "Did you ever do anything about the awful way she treated you?" "How could I?" I asked. "I don't even know her name!" "Oh, I can tell you her name," he said, and gave me both her name—something like Jenny Reilly—and her address. It was one of the small side streets near Saint Nicholas Avenue.

This time I told my brother Uriel the whole story. "You have her name and address?" he asked, "Then what are we waiting for? Let's go!"

My heart was beating as we entered the modest apartment building, found the name "Reilly" on the list, buzzed the buzzer, and walked up to the third floor. The door was opened by a stocky Irishwoman wearing an apron.

Uriel asked, "Are you Mrs. Reilly?" She said "Yes." "Do you have a daughter Jenny?" "Yes." Then he motioned for me to tell my story. And I did, with all the details, trying hard to control the pounding in my chest. Mrs. Reilly listened sadly, like someone who has heard it all before; apparently her daughter had a habit of getting into trouble. Finally, I wound up my narrative with the full dramatic climax that, I thought, would shake the rafters: "And," I took a deep breath, *"it was a Jewish book!"*

But at this Mrs. Reilly looked quite blank. "If it was your book," she said, "Jenny had no right to grab it away from you." I was dumbfounded. Was it conceivable that this whole incident, ugly as it was, had had nothing to do with antisemitism? (To this day I have no satisfactory answer to that question; all I know, from asking the opinions of friends and acquaintances, is that every one of them has very strong convictions on the subject.)

"Well," Mrs. Reilly concluded somewhat wearily, "I'm sorry my daughter behaved so badly. I'll see to it that her father hears about it; you can be sure he will teach her a lesson," and we went home. But Uriel did not have my timidity, and promptly told our father the whole story.

He came into our room the next day and very gently questioned me. He wanted to hear it all from my own mouth. "And where is the book now?" he asked. I burrowed in my drawer, got it out, and handed it to him. And as he took off his glasses and brought the charred book within three inches of his eye to examine it, I could see the flashback spreading across his face, a flashback that I was experiencing at the same time.

As I remembered it, I could not have been more than five years old when one day I heard a commotion of a number of people in the front hall and one voice saying in Yiddish, "We brought Dr. Weinreich." "No, no; you stay here," said my mother to me, and herself ran out to the hall. Later, she explained to me that my father had been caught in the street in the wrong place at the wrong time. A gang of hooligans had been smashing windows of Jewish stores, she said, vandalizing everything in sight, and attacking any Jews who were unlucky enough to be around. My father had been badly beaten up; in addition, his glasses were broken and it seemed that some splinters were lodged in his eye.

Only quite recently did I learn that the events of that day had been a lot more personal and sinister than has been widely known. Incensed by the ongoing vicious harassment of Jewish students at Vilna University, my father took it upon himself to visit the *wojewoda,* or provincial governor, and threaten to get in touch with his contacts in New York (he wrote a regular column for the New York *Forverts*, a Yiddish-language newspaper) creating a scandal that would embarrass the Polish government. As soon as he was out the door the *wojewoda* apparently picked up the phone, and the assault took place on my father's way home.

I remember Dr. Rutshnik, the ophthalmologist, coming every day to examine and treat him. Although it was normal for doctors in general practice to make house calls in Vilna, this did not apply to specialists. Dr. Rutshnik came for two reasons: first, my father's importance as a public figure in his own right; second, his being the son-in-law of Dr. Tsemakh Shabad, who was not only the dean of the Vilna Jewish medical community but highly respected by gentile physicians as well. Even more important, my grandfather (who had himself grown up in the slums of Vilna) was universally revered for the work that he did among the poor, and for his leadership in matters of public health.

Yet in spite of all efforts my father did lose sight of that one eye; and as he got older the other eye degenerated progressively also. For the last twenty or so years of his life this man, whose very soul depended on being submerged in texts, could read only by taking off his glasses and bringing whatever he was reading within three inches of his face.

Now he put his glasses back on and said, "It will be replaced for you, of course." That was his only comment as he took the scorched book with him. The next morning I found waiting for me a brand new clean copy of *di mishpokhe karnovski* by I. J. Singer.

My father died in 1969, when I was forty-one. I went to see my mother then, of course, and she suggested that I look through his things and see if there was anything I would like to keep for myself (Uriel was, by then, no longer alive). Like a fool I bypassed his whole library, knowing that it didn't contain any physics books, which at the time constituted my only interest. What I would give today to have a second chance at that! I did notice, on top of his huge cluttered desk, a pair of paper scissors with very long blades which I used to admire as a child, and which adorn my own desk today. But when I began to browse through the drawers, all I found were bent paper clips, rubber bands sticky with age, unused yellowed stationery, one-cent stamps, and dried-up bottles of ink. Everything was not just old, but *aged,* obsolete, dead. Finally I pulled out the last drawer on the bottom right, which struck me as being unusually light, and found it to be empty except for one single solitary object. It was a copy of I. J. Singer's *di mishpokhe karnovski,* with covers missing, and the rest scorched by a very ancient fire.

4 ❀ LANGUAGE

M y father held a doctorate from the University of
Marburg in what used to be referred to as philology
but would today be called linguistics. Even if his
profession had been different, however, the setting
into which I was born in 1928 was one where the primacy of language was intensely realized. We were Jews in Poland; our natural language was Yiddish, but our linguistic universe was wide
open. Although the immediately surrounding population spoke
Polish, only a decade or so had elapsed since Poland was (by the
Treaty of Versailles) brought back into existence as a sovereign nation; for a century and a half before that, Vilna had existed as a
provincial Russian city. As a consequence, all the adults I knew
were fluent both in Polish and in Russian; in fact, Russian was my
own mother's native tongue. My father, on the other hand, grew

up in a small town in Courland (now part of Latvia) speaking German, historically a dominant language there; at the same time he was familiar both with Russian, the official government language of the time, and Latvian, which the surrounding peasants spoke. As a young adult my mother, too, went to university in Germany and received her doctorate there; in fact, the German language tended generally to be studied by Jewish intelligentsia as an important gateway to European culture. Jews who had themselves come from a religious background—as many had—were, of course, at home with Hebrew, not as a spoken language but as the language of the liturgy and of the Bible. Those who had pursued their religious studies to more advanced levels knew Aramaic as well, Aramaic being the language of most of the Talmud (and, coincidentally, the language that Jesus spoke). And anyone who had gone through the full normal secular sequence of schooling would be conversant with Latin and with Greek.

Altogether, had I known any Bible as a little boy I would have understood perfectly why (according to the first chapter of Genesis) the universe was filled with emptiness until God *spoke*. Before that, I would have said, nothing was happening, not merely because nothing happened to be happening but because the phenomenon known as "time," which endows things with the capacity to happen, did not yet exist. It's not until the third verse, when God *says* "Let there be light," that we first sense the machinery of the universe crunching into gear, signifying that the ticking of time has begun. But whereas I did not, in fact, know any Bible at that age, I did have the impression that, when it came to languages, every Jewish adult knew everything; and one of my most shocking experiences when I arrived in the United States at the age of thirteen was to encounter Jews who actually knew no more than one single language (and it wasn't Yiddish, either).

Our family spent the whole academic year of my sixth birthday in Vienna, away from home, as part of my father's research career. I know that he was very interested in psychoanalysis and went through some analysis himself. His analyst was a pupil of Sigmund Freud, but so was every other analyst in Vienna at that time. More interesting is that he had a close collaboration with

Anna Freud, the master's daughter. My father's special interest, which he shared with her, was the psychology of youth, and when he returned to Vilna he published a book called *der veg tsu undzer yugnt* (*The Pathway to Our Youth*).

Uriel and I were enrolled in kindergarten in Vienna, which I remember fondly because of the toys they had. That everyone spoke German didn't bother us a bit, we just spoke German right along with them even though we didn't know any—but the very fact that I don't remember the learning process means that we picked it up very fast. What stands out in my mind much more was a German-made erector set called Märklin, a marvelous collection of colored metal strips, angles, shafts, wheels, screws, and nuts, out of which one could build anything one wanted. To my technically inclined mind it was an absolute dream, and when we were picked up at the end of the day I could think of nothing else until the next morning when I would get to play with the Märklin set again.

We returned to Vilna in the spring of 1934, and the following fall I started elementary school, the same one in which my mother taught. There were altogether about a dozen secular Yiddish elementary schools in Vilna; ours numbered among its student body a very wide range of backgrounds. There were children of intellectuals—teachers, doctors, lawyers, and engineers—such as Uriel and I were. There were also many lower-class kids from the poor neighborhoods. Although I was not myself a witness to this, I heard that in one early grade, when the teacher asked everyone to tell what their fathers did for a living, the usual series of "My dad is a tailor," "My dad is a teacher," "My dad is a carpenter," "My dad has a drygoods store" also included "My dad is a pickpocket."

The school functioned entirely in Yiddish, with the exception of two subjects—Polish language and Polish history—which were required by law to be taught in Polish. To know Polish was a practical necessity, because that was the language used to communicate at the post office, or with a policeman, or perhaps at the farmers' market—or with the maid at home. In connection with the last, my father liked to recount an episode that happened when I was about four, in which we were all seated at the dinner table when I was sent to ask the maid for some more bread. Although the request was, of course, made to me in Yiddish, I automatically transmitted it to the maid in Polish without—according to my father, who was eavesdropping—being the least bit aware that I had shifted languages.

Naturally, all the stores we patronized were Jewish, so one spoke Yiddish there. If I needed to ask someone in the street for directions, or what time it was, I would approach a Jew and ask in Yiddish. Since Jews constituted between a quarter and a third of the city's population, it was never difficult to locate one, but what is interesting to me today is the certainty we all had that, without being taught, one can recognize a Jew by his or her appearance—a certainty that was apparently borne out by the facts. I'm not sure how this worked, but I do know that when I came to New York I found that it was no longer true: a stranger who "looked like a Jew" could just as well be Italian or Greek!

In May of 1939, when I was in fifth grade, Uriel turned thirteen. As a special birthday present he would get to accompany my father to the International Linguistics Congress in Brussels the following September, first stopping in Copenhagen to visit colleagues and friends. My mother was to accompany them until the beginning of the school year would bring her back, and I was to stay with my grandmother in her summer place in Niemież outside the city, where we had normally been spending our summers. (It is interesting that my family referred to a boy's thirteenth birthday as a "bar–mitzvah," and considered it an important landmark meriting an unusually generous gift, without for a moment attributing any religious significance to it.) My grandmother was uneasy over this plan because she could see the dark clouds on the international horizon, and she had no desire to get stuck with an eleven–year–old boy to care for if war did break out. Consequently, she exacted an absolute promise from my mother to return, by the fastest means available, the moment she received a message to that effect, no questions asked. With this proviso, they took off on August 17, 1939.

My grandmother's message went out unexpectedly soon, on August 23, when Hitler and Stalin signed the nonaggression pact that totally astounded the world; now it was clear that Germany could invade Poland without fear of appreciable resistance there. True to her word, my mother dropped everything and returned. At about the same time, the International Linguistic Congress was cancelled, but my father, always the optimist, figured that he and Uriel could use the opportunity to enjoy some more of Denmark. On September 1, German panzer divisions crossed the Polish frontier, followed on September 17 by the Soviet invasion from the east; the partition of Poland by those two powers was completed on September 29. As a consequence, my father's Polish passport became a meaningless piece of paper, and he, together with his young son, found themselves stateless persons stranded in wartime in a foreign country. Denmark was neutral, however, and my father immediately enrolled Uriel for school. Did he know any Danish? No, but of course he picked it up, adding one more language to his roster.

Vilna being located in the far northeast of what had been Poland, my mother and I now found ourselves under Soviet rule; almost immediately, however (and to everyone's surprise), the Soviets ceded Vilna to nominally neutral Lithuania, which claimed a historic right to the city as its ancient capital. Thus sixth grade began in total turmoil, but soon settled down to a life that, to me at least, did not seem all that different from what it had been before, except that the Jewish community now groaned under the burden of large numbers of refugees who had fled before the Nazis as they advanced. Also, the two subjects of Polish language and Polish history, previously taught in Polish, were replaced by Lithuanian language and Lithuanian history, taught in Lithuanian.

This new curriculum was, however, a lot more problematic, because whereas everyone, both teachers and students, had been pretty fluent in Polish, nobody knew any Lithuanian. As far as the kids were concerned, we essentially hadn't known that such a language existed. The statement we were now often hearing, that even before the war Vilna (now called by its Lithuanian name Vilnius) had had a sizable Lithuanian population, struck us as pure propaganda, since we were unaware of ever in our lives having encountered such people. The reason was that since 1920 the two countries were not speaking to each other (precisely because of the dispute over who owned Vilna) and the border had been sealed. Vilna did, indeed, have a moderately sized Lithuanian minority, but I guess they felt it prudent not to make a show of their ethnicity as long as the Poles were in charge.

So all our teachers now had to register for crash courses in the new official language, and special instructors were imported from Lithuanian-speaking territory to teach both them and the kids. This was hard going for all of us, because Lithuanian is a difficult language: neither Slavic nor Germanic, it is an ancient Indo-European outgrowth, unfamiliar both in vocabulary and morphology. As one might expect, the kids got it a lot faster than the poor adults; nonetheless, it did cast a shadow over my whole sixth grade.

By March of 1940 my father, blocked in his efforts to get home by the fact that he was stateless and not a Vilna native, finally gave up; in his mind, of course, he was kicking himself for not returning the previous August as my mother had. In retrospect, however, it was precisely his optimism that saved our lives: without it, all four of us would have perished in the Holocaust three years later. In the meantime he, along with Uriel, took off for New York instead, desperately hoping that arrangements could be made for us to join them there.

In the meantime, in the spring of 1940, I graduated from elementary school and became eligible for *gimnazye*, or secondary school; but that June, before the new school year began, the Red Army returned, and Lithuania became part of the Soviet Union as one of its constituent republics. Now the pressure was to learn Russian, but that was generally less of a problem since the language was familiar to many people. The only complication was that the alphabet was different, but learning a few new symbols was not that much of a deal—in fact, I found it rather fun.

In September of 1940 I did enroll in *gimnazye*. I remember very little of it, however, because the times were stormy and I did not attend it for very long. Sometime during that summer the Soviets requisitioned the apartment where I had lived all my life;

by then, my mother had already transferred all of my father's books to the YIVO building. His library had been huge: I remember an enormous room, covered with bookshelves from wall to wall and from floor to very high ceiling. I don't know what my mother did with the rest of our belongings, but I know that the two of us moved in with my grandmother. Her apartment was actually quite spacious—it included the rooms where at one time, when he was still alive, my grandfather received his patients—but it was already occupied by a sizable number of people, mostly family and friends who were refugees from German–occupied territory.

The news that my father had succeeded in obtaining American visas for my mother and me came the first week of December, and we took off more or less immediately (I will describe our journey in more detail in a later chapter). I recall saying a quick and peremptory goodbye to my grandmother as we were getting into the taxi. On the way to the station, I noticed that my mother was crying, and when I asked her why, she said "I'm afraid I might never see my mother again." I thought that was preposterous. All this war business was bound to blow over, and we would be back home in no time at all. (My grandmother died with the liquidation of the Vilna ghetto in September 1943.)

After crossing Siberia, Japan, the Pacific Ocean, and the American continent, a journey of which I shall give more details in a later chapter, we reached New York on January 28, 1941. Since the school term was about to begin, my father took me down to the high school the very next day to get me enrolled. I was not quite thirteen at the time, rather young for ninth grade, but my father, in addition to having an academically pushy streak, had a special concern: it was the general policy of the New York schools in dealing with immigrant children who were deficient in English, American history, and civics not to allow them out of elementary school until they had caught up with general American standards. As a result, many of those kids ended up still in elementary school when they had really grown too old for that, in addition to having to suffer the humiliation of repeating over and over again subjects in which their performance had been adequate or better.

So my father decided to do an end run around the system and took me to see Miss Ross, the assistant principal of George Washington High School, to arrange for immediate admission. It will always remain a mystery to me how he managed to talk her into such a totally irregular arrangement when I literally didn't know as much as a single word of English. But he did; and on the first day of the term I took off for school equipped with pencil, notebook, and a note from my father that said "This boy does not understand any English. Please give him all the consideration possible." By the end of that term I was getting good grades in all subjects including English. The following term I started Latin, adding Spanish a year later.

I remember feeling offended when I heard other students in Latin class translating from Latin into English, because what they were doing was converting excellent Latin into terrible English. To my mind, such a degradation might have been excusable when going in the other direction, because inadequate Latin was the best they had available; but English? English is what they knew well! English is what they spoke beautifully and idiomatically! Not, perhaps, as beautifully or idiomatically as Cicero spoke Latin, but at least, for God's sake, take your time and give it a try! Instead, their aim seemed to be merely to demonstrate to the teacher that they had memorized the vocabulary—if indeed they had—and (in the case of the better students) that they could distinguish an accusative from an ablative. Not only weren't they "getting it," but in the process they were insulting language, and by now language was my personal friend.

The fact that I had by that time been exposed, in varying degrees, to perhaps a dozen languages had as its result not so much a knowledge of *languages* as a knowledge of *language*. Language and I were, indeed, friends, a friendship that implied, among other things, a great mutual respect. "Provide me with a fulcrum," Archimedes is supposed to have said, "and I will move the earth." In the same way, I felt that I could always understand a given language by virtue of understanding language in general. This was, of course, an expression of the linguistics in my blood, which I had "inherited" from my father and from Uriel.

Incidentally, I clearly remember how the very first day of Latin class, when we were issued our textbooks, I greedily began to read mine while the other kids were still filling out their cards. The introduction, I found, listed some reasons for studying Latin, among them (a) it helps one with the meaning of English words; (b) it helps one with one's English spelling. I then continued on to the vocabulary list of Lesson 1, which turned out to include the word *exspectare*, "to await," different from its English cognate *both* in meaning *and* in spelling. I decided then and there that the textbook wasn't "getting it" either, since it was obvious to me that the study of Latin was useful for only one purpose, and that was to learn Latin. Language and I had a good laugh over that, which, that evening, we shared with my father and Uriel.

A third of a century later, when I started occasionally accompanying Gerane to Saint Andrew's Episcopal Church in Ann Arbor, one of the things that attracted me most powerfully was that *it was a place of language*. The liturgy beckoned in majestic Elizabethan English, in which it was necessary to invest oneself in order to absorb it properly; and I found myself excellently prepared (and motivated) to make such an investment. Then there were the Bible readings, which were delivered conscientiously, heard attentively, and discussed imaginatively in the sermon that followed. I did not, actually, know much Bible at the time, since our secular Yiddish schools had not placed any emphasis on it; yet the spirit of those texts, due to a peculiar type of osmosis that inevitably takes place when one grows up in a Jewish setting, felt amazingly familiar. It was also exhilarating to recognize that, for example, the English words *Holy, holy, holy* that were always sung as part of the communion service were the same as the Latin *Sanctus, sanctus, sanctus* about which I had learned in my courses in music history in college, and the same also as the Hebrew *kodoysh, kodoysh, kodoysh* that I was somehow aware (correctly) were a central part of some Jewish prayer (though I would not have been able to place it more precisely because of my essentially total ignorance of Jewish liturgy). The additional discovery that "Holy, holy, holy" is actually a quotation from the (Jewish!) prophet Isaiah enhanced this exhilaration further.

The peculiar result of all this was that, rather than being an ignorant newcomer among people who had been born, grew up, and lived their lives as church-going Christians, it was suddenly I who, in many ways, came to be regarded as a knowledgeable expert. What was happening was that my good friend Language had introduced me to *its* good friend, whose name was Religion. God, on the other hand, who appeared to be the cousin of Religion, was still some distance away. It's true that my new friend Religion seemed to talk incessantly about its cousin, but you know how new friends sometimes are.

In 1978, when I turned fifty, I decided that we would have a "real" *seder* meal for Passover, to which I would invite, in addition to our nuclear family and a few close Jewish friends, the rector of Saint Andrew's as well. In preparation, I studied the *haggadah*, the Hebrew seder liturgy, intensively for some months, trying to combine old memories with new understandings. (I also cooked and froze various specialty dishes that I felt to be indispensable.) The seder, which kept going past midnight, was a resounding success (there is a rabbinic rule that the eating must be finished by midnight, but no such restriction applies to the conversation). Early the following year I told the rector that I would like to give a few evening talks at church dealing with the historical relationship between Judaism and Christianity. He was delighted, and scheduled my series, under the title "Our Larger Family," for the six Sunday evenings of Lent; this, too, was successful, with a faithful audience of perhaps a dozen people attending and asking questions.

A year after that—in 1980, when I was fifty-two—I produced another set of six Lenten talks called "Problems of Bible Language and Translation." In spite of the stuffy academic title, an enthusiastic audience similar to the previous year's was there again every Sunday evening. I was elated by my success and by the compliments that I received. Language and I, aided by my new friend Religion, seemed to be heading in a new direction that felt so good that I decided to write a book based on the second set of lectures.

Yet in spite of my great sense of satisfaction, and in spite of the many compliments I received from people to whom I showed the developing manuscript, I felt myself losing momentum. I had no idea what was wrong until one of my friends, having read a few chapters, remarked: "It's awfully good prose, but why are you writing this, and for whom?" It turned out that I had no idea. Sure, it was fun to show off my recently amassed knowledge of both Judaism and Christianity, and to play hide–and–seek with the reader who, I imagined, would always be wondering, "So which flavor is he?" But while writing good prose, I had forgotten what that prose was supposed to say—indeed, had really never clearly known. Something was missing. And then it began to dawn on me that even though my old friend Language had introduced me to my new friend Religion, and the three of us were having a ball, perhaps that cousin whom Religion was always talking about might actually be playing a much more central role in all of this than I had originally understood.

The Bible begins with language; according to the first chapter of Genesis, the universe was filled with emptiness until God *spoke*; but, I was beginning to wonder, would there have been anyone to speak had there not been God?

5 ❧ SELF-DISCIPLINE

Since I have now mentioned my mother and her family on a number of occasions, it seems appropriate to devote the next two chapters to a more formal introduction.

On what we call "The picture wall" in our house, there is a posed studio portrait of my mother and her two brothers from around 1915, thirteen years before I was born. Yasha, the middle child and in later years my favorite uncle, looks to be fourteen; the youngest brother Zhozya, whom I never met, appears to be ten or eleven. That would make my mother Regina seventeen. Indeed, that is the judgment of neutral observers when I ask them to estimate the age of the slightly overweight red-haired young woman in the picture; but when I look at it I see my mother, which in my eyes automatically places her in her middle thirties. The red hair is also mostly in my mind, of course, since the actual photograph is monochrome sepia.

Three spaces to the right on the same wall is an unposed portrait of my mother as my children remember her: a white-haired
lady in her seventies, her brow furrowed in deep thought in a
characteristic gesture that I knew well. Again, however, when I
look at the picture I see a woman in her middle thirties with
bright red hair. In both cases, the illusion is so powerful that I
have not been able to shake it.

I remember, as a child, walking into stores with my mother
and noticing people respectfully making room for us; sometimes
I would even overhear someone whisper: "That's Dr. Shabad's
daughter, you know." The reference was, of course, to my grandfather, who was universally known and universally revered. Born
in 1863, he emerged from a very modest Jewish family to become
a fully accredited medical doctor, an unusual feat in his generation; this was followed by postgraduate research in Switzerland
on the subject of diabetes that resulted in the publication of a
number of pioneering papers in Russian and European journals.
Back in Vilna, he devoted himself to issues of public health and
to work among the poor, quickly becoming a high-profile community leader; and even though by the 1930s, which is the time
that I remember, there must have been close to a hundred Jewish
medical doctors in regular practice in Vilna, Dr. Shabad always remained the dean of that community.

My grandparents, known to us kids as "Zeyde" and "Boba,"
had a spacious apartment, half of which served as Zeyde's office,
and the rather dark waiting room (so I remember it) was always
full of people most of whom were shabbily dressed. I was told that
he received everyone, habitually assuring them that if they weren't
able to pay the rather nominal fee it could "wait until a later time."
When he wasn't receiving patients or attending meetings or making hospital visits he was, as likely as not, making house calls
somewhere in the slums, an area he knew well because he was
born and bred there himself. More than fifty years later I met an
old lady in New York who, when she found out who I was, burst
into tears: shortly after her father had died of cholera in the First
World War, her mother, now the sole sustenance of six little children, contracted the same deadly and terribly contagious disease,

and no doctor would come near her—until Dr. Shabad heard about it, began to visit daily, taught the family essential techniques of personal hygiene, paid for all medications, nursed her back to health, and then refused to give her a bill.

Within our family, however, it was not Zeyde but Boba who was the seat of power. Boba was the oldest of six daughters of an aristocratic and wealthy Vilna family and in her youth was stunningly beautiful to boot. She was married quite young, being only nineteen or twenty when my mother, her oldest child, was born, whereas Zeyde was by then thirty-five. Because of this age difference we always felt him to be a little distant, although he was pleasant and kind and we loved him very much. By contrast Boba, far from being distant, was deeply involved in our day-to-day life and seemed to be regarded by my mother as the ultimate authority on everything.

Zeyde and Boba were strong believers in the supreme virtue of tilling the soil as a way of coming close to nature and therefore close to what, in some sense, human beings were meant to be (I say "in some sense" because neither one of them professed any religion in the conventional sense of the word). Although the notion of the "noble peasant" was generally popular among Russian intellectuals of that day, it took on a special meaning for Jews since, for historical reasons, agriculture as a Jewish occupation was comparatively rare. That, presumably, was the reason that my uncle Yasha was packed off to Germany to study modern agronomy and, when he returned, was established on a piece of land a few miles from Vilna to develop new and more productive methods of farming (his early tomatoes soon became famous throughout the city).

I strongly suspect that the same philosophy led my grandparents to send my mother to do graduate work in botany at the University of Frankfurt-am-Main, an unusually ambitious activity for a young Jewish woman from that part of the world. Yet that particular university was itself quite unusual. In the first place it was brand new, having had its official founding ceremony as recently as 1914. Second, it was not only new but thoroughly modern in every respect, including numbering one hundred women in its first student body of six hundred or so—an astronomically high proportion for a European university of that time.

As I imagine it, saying "No" to Boba was not an option, yet in their own way both Yasha and my mother rebelled. In Yasha's case, the rebellion consisted in getting a German girlfriend in Berlin pregnant, which required his parents in Vilna to arrange for a hasty marriage until the baby was born and an equally hasty divorce soon afterwards. Interestingly, although Yasha himself subsequently showed only a limited interest in the boy, this was not at all true of Boba, who cherished him as her first grandson and had him spend summers with her as soon as he was old enough to travel alone. She also kept up cordial relations with his mother and, I assume, helped her financially to learn a trade and become self-supporting. In later years she was a successful corsetière, first in Berlin, then in Paris; and her son—four years older than Uriel—was our beloved summer playmate.

In my mother's case, the rebellion was more complex. First of all, she fell in love with my father and insisted on marrying him in 1920, having already begun her studies in Germany (I infer this from the fact that she continued at the university under her maiden name). As far as I know, the wedding did not take place in Vilna (as her parents would surely have preferred) but somewhere in Germany, where at the time my father was also studying, though at a different university. Second, from the moment she successfully finished her doctoral work and returned to Vilna around 1925 (Uriel was born in 1926), her botany PhD was, except for the bare fact of its existence, never heard from again—in striking contrast to that of her husband, who was, in my memory, universally addressed as "Dr. Weinreich." Instead, she became a career elementary–school art teacher, a position that brought her a great deal of satisfaction and fulfillment, and in which she continued up to the moment we left Vilna late in 1940. My mother also got much enjoyment out of needlework of every kind and was seldom without her knitting, crocheting, or embroidering project.

Some of my earliest memories of my mother are of her drawing, with pastel pencils, on a large pad that she held gently and lovingly in her lap. She presented Uriel and me with sets of watercolors at an early age and tried to teach us NOT TO SQUEEZE the brush down on the paint or on the paper but to use its point gently and delicately, carefully twirling the stem to make the bristles absorb just the right amount of pigment. When she herself did it, it was absolutely beautiful, and I could watch in fascination for hours as stunning textures of blue and orange and green flowed effortlessly from her brush and blended on the moistened paper. But when she left me to work on my own the results were always totally discouraging, and within minutes I had jammed my brush down so hard that its ferrule was filled with solid paint and the bristles stuck out in all directions like an ugly mutated porcupine. The result was that I tended quickly to lose patience and sweep the whole paint set off onto the floor.

Today I would say that there was something seriously flawed in my mother's approach. She was trying to hold me to standards that I was too young to satisfy, with the result that my frustration far outstripped any possible satisfaction or enjoyment. Indeed, I remember watching her a generation later with my own children and experiencing the same old feeling when, upon being presented with a new masterpiece of refrigerator art, she would always respond with "That's beautiful, dear, but wouldn't it be better if this section here had a bit more purple in it?" For God's sake, I thought, can't you ever accept anything without pointing out a defect? To her, however, it was less a matter of finding fault than of not wasting a possible opportunity for improvement. Indeed, in a conversation that we once had adult to adult, she explicitly and emphatically articulated the principle that working toward attainable goals is a waste of time: human beings should always concentrate their efforts on unattainable goals. That way, whatever you do accomplish, you are always assured that it was the very best of which you were capable. This was the approach that Boba had not only always taught her, but herself practiced with ruthless dedication. As far as she was concerned, the fact that it left one in a state of permanent frustration was unimportant compared to the self–discipline that it helped to develop. And self–discipline was the name of the game.

The idea of self-discipline as a good in itself is, of course, very old. Many Eastern religions place it high on their list of virtues, and the ancient Greeks—both heroes and philosophers—did their part to extol it; it is not surprising, therefore, that it early became an important component of the culture of Christianity as well. This is shown, for example, by the development of a large and important monastic movement, composed of people who took self-discipline for the greater glory of God as their life's vocation. Yet the great problem with self-discipline—which by definition ought to have some direct or, at least, indirect purpose—is the ease with which it can slip into the much darker practice of self-denial or self-deprivation, which serves no purpose except to punish oneself. In the case of Christianity, this shows itself not only in some monastic practices of the hair-shirt variety but in the teaching emanating from countless pulpits over the centuries that somehow enjoyment of life is intrinsically sinful.

How this happened is, to my mind, something of a mystery. Self-deprivation is certainly not a central component of Old Testament doctrine, nor will an unprejudiced reader of the Gospels find much of it in Jesus's own teaching. So, for example, few would interpret the *Beatitudes*—"Blessed are the poor in spirit, for theirs is the kingdom of heaven" and so on—as a directive to his listeners to try to make their lives as miserable as possible, rather than being a simple promise of hope to those whose present misery is not of their own making. At the same time, the glimpses we get of Jesus's own style of life show him, for example, at a wedding in Cana of Galilee, where there was apparently so much happy drinking and carousing that the wine ran out, whereupon Jesus miraculously caused the supply to be replenished—not an act of one who believes in self-deprivation for its own sake.

In fact, it seems to me that the Christian affinity for what became known as "mortification of the flesh" did not originate in Jesus's teaching at all, but in a combination of the then current popular philosophical culture of the Hellenistic world with a developing Christian sensitivity toward the concept of original sin, as we talked about it in an earlier chapter. The first of these had as a cardinal principle the fundamental inferiority of the human body and its "passions" (that is, feelings) to "higher things" that could be attained by the practice of philosophy after all passions had been subdued. The second extended that into a doctrine of essential human worthlessness and the virtue of undergoing suffering and deprivation in order to become one with Christ on the cross. Somewhat paradoxically, however, I don't see either one of those as particularly Christian, much less biblical.

With regard to inferiority of bodily passions, the Greek philosophical ideal was, indeed, to free oneself of them and to act always in accordance with "wise," that is, fully rational, analysis (the modern dictum never to hit one's child in anger is a vestige of that type of thinking). But the God described in the Old Testament (which was, after all, Jesus's God) is not like that at all. On the contrary, God is the prototype of a *passionate* being: loving, gracious, compassionate, on occasion angry but always apt to change his mind before punishment is actually exacted. And what we know of Jesus is similar: a man full of kindness, compassion, and love, surely not one to hide his feelings even though it occasionally leads him to fly off the handle.

As to the second factor—the belief in essential human worthlessness, and the desire to undergo suffering and deprivation in order to become one with Christ on the cross—let me just say that, in my understanding, "becoming one with Christ on the cross" is simply not something to which a Christian is called. As I see it, Christ did not die on the cross in order to suffer for the sake of suffering. Rather, *he died for a profound purpose,* and my understanding of that purpose makes it difficult to see how it would be furthered by making myself miserable in addition. In my opinion Christianity does, indeed, call us to certain tasks, and those tasks often do require a lot of self-discipline; but—as far as I am able to grasp—self-deprivation and self-punishment are not part of that requirement and all too often function merely as excuses for wallowing in our own sense of worthlessness.

Boba herself, I expect, would have been taken aback at the suggestion that her approach to life showed Christian influences; indeed, it would have been hard to prove, since in the latter part of the nineteenth century this manner of thinking was very much in the air. It was, after all, the era of *movements* and of *causes*. Romanticism, which had begun by exalting illustrious individuals who through profound intuition and creative willpower could control the direction of the world, gradually shifted its attention to mass movements that, in the service of some great ideal, could do the same thing, provided its members subordinated their own lives to "The Cause" by cultivating their individual dedication and self-discipline. Not only socialism and communism developed on this basis but also, on the Jewish scene, Zionism and Yiddishism. Yet I am personally convinced that, tracing this worldview back through European cultural history, its medieval Christian roots would quickly come to the fore.

Be that as it may, Boba's allegiance to this way of thinking was absolute. I never in my life saw her exhibit any real passion, never witnessed her laughing or crying; she never hugged me in her arms or kissed me tenderly or expressed either approval or disapproval in any but cold and measured terms. To the world, and especially perhaps to the inhabitants of the Vilna ghetto into which the Jews were driven soon after the start of the German occupation in 1941, she was a woman of iron will and towering integrity, a pillar of self-discipline who, when the time came to die, would know how to die. But to us, her family, she represented at the same time those darker dimensions: the need to exercise one's willpower not merely *even if* it hurts but *especially* then; the steely contempt for any activity directed toward simple pleasure; and the lofty pride of being independent of the weakness of human passions, which necessarily consigned love, the chief of those passions, to a lesser rank.

In fact, it's a miracle that my mother did not grow up acting the same way but, while she too was not likely to laugh or cry with any intensity, her love and devotion to her children was unmistakable. Whenever I had trouble falling asleep, for example, I knew I could count on her to sit (for hours if necessary) on the edge of my bed stroking my hair, making me comfy in every way, until rest finally overtook me. I can even recall her singing to me when I was very young, in spite of her not really being able to sing at all. On the minus side, she was forever taking my temperature at every sniffle and keeping me home from school for a week if I had a "fever" of as much as half a degree. I was, in other words, profoundly loved but also overprotected and spoiled. Perhaps my mother was trying to make up for the opposite treatment I got from Boba, who was not exactly mean but mercilessly strict; what's more, whenever they were both present it was Boba who was in charge and calling the shots.

Incidentally, my mother also had an exceptionally close relationship with her students. While teachers were generally spoken to with the courtesy title *Lerer* or *Lererin* (Yiddish for "teacher," masculine or feminine) followed by a last name, my mother was universally known as *Lererin Regine* rather than *Lererin Weinreich* as a token of special warmth and love. The result of this closeness was that her students often went to her with their personal problems, sometimes long after they had graduated, and in some cases even visited her grave.

When the war made us settle in New York in 1941 my mother, after some years at loose ends, finally found something to do when her aunt Nyuta started a business in ladies' dresses catering to well–to–do Polish refugees. Nyuta was Boba's youngest sister, only two or three years older than my mother herself; she had grown up in Warsaw in rich and refined Polish society, married a successful attorney, and had two handsome children, a boy and a girl roughly the ages of Uriel and me. When the war came they managed to escape and reach New York, but their life was destroyed: Nyuta's attorney husband, now about fifty and without any knowledge of English, tried hard to pass some low–level accounting examinations that would allow him to earn a meager living but had a heart attack and died, leaving Nyuta—used to a life of luxury and high society—as sole breadwinner. Very enterprisingly, she began to shop for designer dresses at reduced prices and sell them to fellow refugees from Warsaw who could recognize good style. Her apartment became a salon where genteel ladies came to speak elegant Polish, be served black coffee in fine porcelain cups, reminisce about the good old days, complain about their husbands and children, and be fitted with exquisite designer apparel. In this setting, my mother became the chief (and only) fitter and seamstress, diagnosing and executing whatever alterations were required.

At first my mother was reluctant to take on such a job. Although very fond of Nyuta, who long ago had been her playmate in their common Russian–speaking childhood, she did not feel herself part of the elegant Warsaw set, and her Polish, though reasonably fluent, was certainly not up to high society standards. On top of that, she had no experience at all with the kind of sewing where a mistake can cost many hundreds of dollars. But her artist's instinct for the mechanics of textiles and the complex geometries of the human body was apparently superb, which often enabled her, with a slight tuck here and a minor adjustment there, to turn a poorly hanging garment into dazzling haute couture. Soon she was sewing things on her own, first for herself and friends, in later years much more so for her daughters–in–law. She told me once that whenever she went to get material for a pattern she habitually bought a quarter of a yard less than nominally required, confident that she could be more clever in the layout—and this in spite of the fact that the patterns of her pieces always matched perfectly at the seams, something the directions seldom called for. I can still see her at her large table, her brow furrowed in deep thought in that characteristic gesture that I knew so well, while her gently moving spread–out fingertips made creases and bulges magically disappear. At such moments it was obvious that this woman, removed from her birthplace by half a world, immersed in unfamiliar languages, and surrounded by a foreign culture, was nonetheless supremely at home.

At the age of seventy–five, five years after the death of her husband, she was diagnosed with abdominal cancer. I visited her in the hospital in New York a number of times, once just after the operation that was considered successful. Among the many subjects that we talked about, my mother mentioned her admiration for the cemetery in Ann Arbor where Alisa, my first wife, was buried; unlike those in New York, with their seemingly endless straight rows of stones extending to the horizon, Forest Hill is set in a wooded and hilly area beautifully laid out in curved lines on a much smaller scale. I asked whether she would like to be buried there too, a suggestion that she enthusiastically embraced. She also had a special request: since her mother, who had perished with the Vilna ghetto and been buried in a mass grave three decades earlier, had no marker of her own, she would like her gravestone to include Boba's memorial as well.

Within days her condition appeared to be worsening again, to the point that a second operation was indicated. I was not in New York for that but spoke to the surgeon on the telephone minutes after he came out of the operating room, and he sounded dazed: never in his long career had he seen a cancer of equal virulence. Ten days after all visible traces had been removed, he told me, the abdominal cavity was again filled to the brim, so there was no point in doing anything except closing up the incision. Clearly, I thought, Boba's daughter was exercising Boba's self-discipline: when the time came to die, she knew how to die. A few days later she was gone.

We buried her under a large shade tree in Forest Hill Cemetery in Ann Arbor, in the presence of her nearest and dearest, and one year later (as is the Jewish custom) we set the stone. Except for her dates—*17.IX.1898–4.VI.1974*—written in a form comprehensible in either language, most of it is in Yiddish; translated, it reads REGINE WEINREICH (LERERIN REGINE), DAUGHTER OF STEFAYNYE–SHIFRE SHABAD WHO PERISHED WITH THE VILNA GHETTO ON SEPTEMBER 23, 1943. At the very end is a short English inscription, quoting the title she had inherited from her mother and by which, at her request, she was always known to her grandchildren:

REGINA WEINREICH

(BOBA)

May her soul, and the souls of all the departed, by the mercy of God rest in peace.

6 ❧ **INCARNATION**

Continuing, as promised, with the introduction of my mother's family: Some time around 1930, my maternal grandparents (or Zeyde and Boba, as we called them) moved from a third–floor apartment directly across the street from ours to one that was not only at street level but closer to the center of town, where the terrain was relatively flat. The reason was that Zeyde, who was pushing seventy, found it increasingly difficult to negotiate the steep hill along which our street, *groys-pohulanke*, ran. Yet as Doctor Shabad who made a lot of house and hospital calls, and as Doctor Shabad the public figure who had to attend a lot of meetings, he needed to traverse that hill several times every day.

Soon after that, around 1932, Boba and Zeyde invested in twenty-five acres of farmland in a village called Niemież about

54

five miles from Vilna, fenced it in with a wooden fence, and built a summer dwelling on it large enough for themselves, our parents, and us two children. The idea was that Zeyde could now travel to the city every day but spend his summer nights peacefully in the country air. For this purpose they also bought a private horsedrawn victoria that would provide him with transportation to and from Niemież as well as taking him from one place in the city to another without needing to hail a cab every time. In the winter, of course, we all reverted to urban life.

Zeyde's personal needs were not, however, the only reason for acquiring the farm. There was also both my grandparents' Tolstoyan belief—already mentioned in the previous chapter—that agriculture is, if not the only worthwhile human occupation, at least a centrally important one. Because of this my mother's younger brother Yasha had been sent to Germany in the 1920s to study agronomy and was upon his return installed on a leased farm, considerably larger than the one in Niemież, to do his thing. Although I gather that he ran the enterprise well, he was nonetheless a bachelor and known as something of a playboy, and whenever we visited him there was apt to be an unknown good-looking but heavily made-up woman keeping him company.

Uriel and I were profoundly in love with Yasha who, while chronologically only three years younger than our mother, was himself in many ways a boy and encouraged us to do exciting and forbidden things. So, for example, he once demonstrated that kerosene, such as was used in the lamps on his farm (there was no electricity either there or in Niemież), is not really very flammable in the absence of a wick; he did this by spilling some liquid out of the reservoir of his lamp onto the linoleum floor and putting a match to it. He was, of course, right, but at home any experiment involving kerosene and matches would have been absolutely and unequivocally forbidden, so Yasha always strictly enjoined us not to tell Boba, his mother, what we had been up to.

Even worse was the fact that he allowed us to play with his pair of service revolvers (like all young men in Poland, he had been through two years of compulsory military service). In fact it was done rather safely: he first made sure that the guns were unloaded; then explained that, while we play, we must *never ever* point them at anyone; and finally he kept an eagle eye on us until the revolvers were safely back in his hands. Again, he emphasized that under no circumstances were we to tell Boba. We did not, of course, consciously betray him, but did naïvely share with our mother the news of our exciting adventure, which she promptly transmitted to Boba (I gather that, as the eldest child, she had always been the "good girl" in the family). Although it was not done within our earshot, Yasha apparently got a good dressing down for the gun incident, because in spite of our fervent requests it was never repeated.

When I was very small, our family regularly rented a cottage near Yasha's farm as a place to spend summer vacations, but when Zeyde and Boba acquired Niemież that became unnecessary. In addition to saving money, the new arrangement freed my mother from constant babysitting duty because in Niemież Boba was, essentially, always there. The way it actually worked out was that my mother, all her life a strong walker, spent most of her summer nights in Niemież and daily went into the city on foot (a ten-mile round trip); whereas my father mostly stayed in the city but came out from time to time—sometimes walking like my mother but mostly taking the bus that ran along the highway a few times daily.

Sadly, however, Zeyde, who may have provided the original impetus for the Niemież farm, never got to enjoy it very much. Shortly after its acquisition he fell ill with gangrene in his foot and, although his leg was eventually amputated, he never made it home from the hospital and died before reaching seventy-one. Ironically, also, the victoria that was meant to ferry him around was stolen soon after we got it.

Uriel and I, on the other hand, flourished in the country: we ran around barefoot all summer and mixed it up with the peasant kids. I in particular was friends with Zbyszek, the young son of the caretaker couple, and we did a lot of playing together. His father had a bit of a drinking problem, and it was said among the peasants that he periodically went to the priest to confess, each time swearing on the crucifix to lay off the booze permanently from then on. Whenever the priest came up in conversation, the peasants crossed themselves and murmured something about *Jezus Chrystus*. I once asked Zbyszek what that phrase meant, and he explained that *Jezus Chrystus* was the name of God.

But when I mentioned to my father in passing that "their God" was named Jezus Chrystus, he said that was not exactly correct. "So who *is* their God?" I asked, and my father replied, "Their God is, well, God." I have no idea how conversant my father actually was with the details of Christian theology, but today I have to say that his answer, addressed to a boy of six, wasn't half bad: "Their God is, well, God."

If you ask Christians today who Jesus Christ is, my guess is that they would say, not "Jesus Christ is God," but "Jesus Christ is *the Son of* God," leaving for another day the problem of what exactly that means. For that matter, if you ask a group of Christians, "Do you believe that Jesus Christ was the Son of God?" most will say "Yes," some will say "No," but very, very few will say "I don't understand what you mean"—though in fact they themselves would find it hard to throw any light on the subject. Yet few concepts of Christianity are more central.

To clarify some background: In the Jewish tradition God not only does not have any sons but cannot have any sons (or daughters), because the relationship between parents which gives rise to offspring is understood to be by its nature a relationship between members of the same species; and God's uniqueness—the first article of Jewish faith—means that there can be no one else of the same species. But when Christians say that Jesus is the Son of God, they mean something radically different: although there is no "spouse" who belongs to the same species as God—still admitted to be impossible—there was, definitely, a pseudosexual action of God by virtue of which a human female, Mary the daughter of Joachim and Anne, became pregnant, giving birth to the baby Jesus nine months later. Nothing like that, Christians believe, ever took place before, or will take place again, but it did take place that one time. What's more, unlike the case of Zeus making Danaë pregnant with baby Perseus, or Leda with baby Helen, Jesus is not merely a baby but is, in the words of the Nicene Creed (an ancient liturgical recitation) "eternally begotten of the Father, . . . true God from true God. . . . For us and for our salvation he came down from heaven; by the power of the Holy Spirit he became incarnate from the Virgin Mary, and was made man."

Became incarnate. So Jesus Christ is both: God and man. And right away it becomes obvious that the incarnation is a very, very difficult concept to understand. Apparently, unlike Perseus or Helen, Jesus Christ is neither a human being that happens to have some divine properties nor a god who happens to have some human properties. According to classical Christian theology, he is neither fifty/fifty, nor eighty/twenty, nor twenty/eighty. He is a hundred/a hundred, wholly God and wholly man.

For some reason that I do not quite understand, Christians have historically expended a great deal of effort to explain this idea away, mostly in one of two ways. First, one can try to "humanize" Jesus and play down his divine side, by thinking of him as basically a great teacher of profound moral values. He taught that people should love one another. He taught that they should share what they have with others less fortunate than themselves. He taught that God should be worshiped in love, rather than in meaningless ceremony. In a word (so goes this interpretation), Jesus was a wonderful human being who, by his preaching and example, called his fellow men and women toward a better and fuller humanity, somewhat like Socrates, or Confucius, or others whom history has revealed to us; and his supposed divinity was merely illusion. This is the point of view often taken today by strongly "liberal" branches of Christianity.

Second, one can push the "wholly God and wholly man" conundrum the other way by "*de*humanizing" Jesus, saying that he was and remains God, pure and simple; today, this is indeed the interpretation of some very "conservative" branches of Christianity. It's true that he had an earthly ministry during a few stormy years of the first century, somewhat the way a king might dress up as a commoner and go out among his people: certainly it's a wonderful way of increasing contact with them, but it doesn't make him any less a king and not a commoner. To people who are committed to this view, every word that Jesus spoke must be taken at face

value, because God is omniscient and does not lie. Further, it is totally out of the question to imagine Jesus confused, or forgetful, or
ignorant of the future, or losing his temper, as we ourselves may
do from time to time at the end of a hard day; such behavior is
just not consistent with his being divine. In a word, for those who
accept this view Jesus is simply God, and it is his humanity that
must be seen as illusion.

In my opinion neither the humanization nor the dehumanization of Jesus is at all helpful, let alone necessary. What is, by
contrast, fascinating and important are the consequences that the
incarnation brought with it.

If this question is asked historically rather than theologically,
then the answer, though not entirely simple, is nonetheless
straightforward. We know that Judaism originated as a tribal religion, in that being a Jew has always involved a lot more than just
religion: Jews share a history, a culture, in some settings even a
language, which sets them apart. Although conversion to Judaism
is certainly not an impossibility, it remains true that in the huge
majority of cases a person is a Jew because of being born into a
Jewish family or, in larger terms, into the Jewish tribe. If Jewish
parents neglect to circumcise their son, the boy becomes an un-
circumcised Jew, but a Jew nevertheless. If a Jew decides to be baptized and embrace Christianity, he or she becomes a baptized Jew,
but a Jew in spite of it. I quote these last two cases in particular
because both have historically been considered major affronts to
traditional Jewish values, affronts whose intensity can only be understood if one sees them as being committed, not by a *former* Jew,
but by someone who still belongs to the tribe.

The reason that this aspect of Judaism is historically important
for Christianity is that, by the time of Christ, much of the gentile
Mediterranean world was ripe for the kind of religion which, in the
abstract, Judaism offers; specifically, this means a religion guided
by what I call the *Sinai Principle* (because it was, according to Jewish
self-understanding, revealed at Mount Sinai to the motley crowd
that was on its way to becoming the Jewish people). The Sinai
Principle is the tenet that *the supreme power that governs the universe
physically also governs it morally;* and its corollary that, since morality

fundamentally operates on an individual level, *the supreme power that governs the universe also cares passionately about every single one of us.*

The problem was that for a religion to be appealing is not the same as for it to be accessible. Because of the tribal nature of Judaism, an interested gentile could not simply come along and join. Rabbinic procedures for becoming a Jew were strongly discouraging, often leaving a would-be convert with the impression that Jews only believed in a *modified* Sinai Principle, in which the phrase "cares passionately about every single one of *us*" is replaced by "cares passionately about one of *them.*" And that's where Christianity came in: while subscribing to the same fundamental idea of an all-powerful but also all-caring and all-loving God, the new religion was the opposite of tribal in that, through baptism, every person enters Christianity *as an individual.* And if the Jewish God could sometimes seem pretty distant and preoccupied with the arcane business of running the universe, there was always Jesus, open to everybody (yes, even gentiles!), concerned with everybody (yes, even sinners!), loving everybody (yes, even me!), welcoming everybody into the sacred fellowship of the Sinai Principle (though not, to be sure, under that name). In this way people began to flock to be saved from what they felt had been their previous life of sin, and *Jezus Chrystus* became the name of God.

That is, more or less, the *historical* picture as I understand it. The *theological* picture, on the other hand, is much more complex and, to my mind, much more fascinating, because it initiates the exploration of the incredibly daring idea that there exists, between God and humanity, a dimension of continuity that had not until then been explicitly recognized. The fact that Jesus Christ, himself somehow a part of God, used the human Mary as a conduit to humanity means that there is a part of God capable of literally experiencing what we experience, sharing in our gladness, joy, and hope, as well as in our sorrow, grief, and despair. In relation to us, it puts God (through Christ) less in the position of a master than of an older loving and sympathetic brother.

At the same time, the God-humanity continuum opened by the incarnation works in the opposite direction. In spite, for example, of the often heard injunction that "it is wrong to play God," doesn't life, in fact, force us to play God over and over again? A surgeon compelled to make a rapid decision that may determine whether another human being lives or dies; a parent of small children, whose hands daily hold the power to help them grow into creative and loving adults or into others who live out their lives confused, frightened, and angry; is that not playing God? In fact, each one of us who is involved in an intimate and vulnerable relationship with another human being wields, at each moment, such enormous power to create or to destroy that to describe it as "playing God" is neither an exaggeration nor a metaphor but an absolutely literal description. And while it is a frequently held opinion that God wants nothing else of us but to wait for and follow orders, I believe that (as is true for any other good parent) God's greatest pleasure comes from our embracing the duty of growing up—not, of course, by shedding our limitations and becoming divine, but by being aware of our limitations and acting responsibly within them. That is the gift of the incarnation.

Which brings me back to my uncle Yasha: On June 22, 1941 (six months after my mother and I had left Vilna), Hitler's armies began to move eastward into Soviet territory, and it was clear that the Germans would be in Vilna in a matter of days. Many Jews packed up what they could and fled east, but Boba firmly announced that she was staying. "I am an old woman," she declared (she was in her early sixties, more than a decade younger than I am now), "what can they do to me?" A native of Vilna who had lived most of her life there, for her that was it: she would remain with her people. But childlike and somewhat irresponsible Yasha, who was thirty-nine, felt differently: together with his foreman Velvl and Velvl's teenage son Khayim–Dovid and adolescent daughter Nekhe, he packed a wagon high with belongings, harnessed the two best horses, and headed east.

At that time, my mother and I were already safely in New York with my father and Uriel, and there was no communication with Russia possible for the next few years. By the time contact was reestablished, Yasha was a major in the Red Army, heavily decorated in some of the bloodiest fighting around Stalingrad, and stationed in Kuybyshev deep in Russia. As I recall it, there was a period of time when we were getting his letters (though with immense delays) but he was not getting ours, which he interpreted as meaning that his sister was refusing to communicate with him because he had abandoned their mother in the jaws of the enemy. (Boba was, in fact, shot and buried in a mass grave at the liquidation of the Vilna ghetto, on September 23, 1943.) Yasha repeated in every letter that, when they passed through Niemież while fleeing Vilna, he stopped at Boba's house and banged on the door and kept calling, but she must have been afraid to open thinking that it was the Germans, so that he had no choice but to continue on. Although my mother, bless her, took that account at face value, it always seemed to me that its details were suspiciously vague.

At length the Red Army, together with the Allied forces coming from the west, were victorious, and Yasha returned to his native Vilna, where he settled down once more, this time not as a farmer but as a Soviet civil servant. Unfortunately, I never did get to see him again; even though I headed for Vilna in 1960, the very summer the Soviets opened the city up to tourists, he had died two years earlier.

During that first visit, I did run into perhaps half a dozen prewar friends who had, after assorted hair-raising adventures, successfully returned home when peace was established. It was also the occasion on which I first met Sonya, the woman Yasha married after his return, who had immigrated to Vilna from the interior of Lithuania and been employed by him as a private teacher of Lithuanian. Khayim-Dovid, the son of Yasha's foreman Velvl (Velvl himself had died in Siberia, where the family had been evacuated during the war), was now the president of a local collective farm, and he drove Alisa and me in his official jeep to Niemież where the house of my grandparents (minus the fence, which had been burned for fuel during the war) was still standing and being used as a school. Although the teacher there did not exactly receive us with open arms (those were, after all, still the Soviet days, and he obviously worried about what might happen to him if he had contact with foreign visitors), the general layout of the farm was just as I recalled it, which brought me a certain amount of the pleasure of remembrance. All in all, however, it was only a two-day visit to Vilna, and I don't believe that I myself was then (at the age of thirty-two) capable of the openness and intimacy that the occasion demanded. As a result, I tended to act as an outsider, and was treated as an outsider in return.

I returned to Vilna for my second (and presumably last) time, in the company of Gerane, our daughter Becky, and her partner Tara, in the summer of 1996. I was now more than twice as old as during my previous visit, and much had happened in all of our lives in the interim, so that Sonya and I, in particular, were able to communicate on a much more trusting and intimate level. Apparently she had been a young bride in the interior of the country when, at the outbreak of the war, she lost her first husband; she then spent the rest of the war as a widow, hiding out as all Jews were compelled to do, and ending up in Vilna. But when Yasha, too, returned to Vilna, she fell head over heels in love with the handsome officer ("Major Shabad was so beautiful!" she repeatedly told me, "so beautiful!") and, hearing that he was looking for a private teacher of Lithuanian, jumped at the opportunity; she would have married him in an instant if he had only declared his love for her, but apparently, even though in his heart he reciprocated her feelings, his past experiences impeded him. Finally, one day when he came for his lesson, he said to her, "Sofya Abramovna" (they spoke Russian and therefore addressed each other with a patronymic), "would you please take a telegram to your sister in Kaunas?" She was surprised, but dutifully took up a pad of paper and a pencil. "Shabad proposed." he dictated with a straight face, "I accepted. Am very happy. Letter follows. Signed, Sonya." She did then accept on the spot, and in her story I recognized my beloved playful uncle. Then we both cried.

That proposal took place in 1946, and after that their devotion to each other was absolute; in her stories I could see the man I had loved half a century before, but although he had his old sense of humor he was also completely changed in being grown up, responsible, and capable of deep and intense love for a

woman instead of relying on the transient affairs that had characterized his life before the war. One evening a week (I well recalled him always organizing his life with great regularity and
precision) he went to his chess club to play, something I was surprised to learn because in spite of his superior intelligence I had
never known him to have the concentration which that game de-
mands. It was on one of those weekly evenings in 1958, hunched
over the chessboard in a difficult game, that Yasha had a heart attack, and by the time they took him to the hospital he was dead.
(At the time, Sonya was convinced that she could not live without him and would surely be dead too a short time later, but as
sometimes happens in a very happy marriage she outlived him
by forty years.) When, I asked myself, had he so radically
changed? It is a commonplace, of course, that war has dramatic
effects on people, but knowing my uncle as I did, and knowing
that in his late thirties he was still that familiar, wonderful, exciting, but somewhat irresponsible little boy, I had a strong hunch
that in his case there must have been some particular moment
that wrought such a transformation.

Of course in externals, too, my second visit to Vilna was quite
different. On the one hand, Lithuania was now an independent
democratic state, the city had expanded and was generally pros-
perous-looking, and we could move around much more freely; on
the other hand, not only Yasha, Velvl his foreman, and Khayim-
Dovid but a number of other characters in this story were now
dead (including my mother). Velvl's daughter Nekhe, however, a
young adolescent at the time of the war's outbreak and so more
or less my age, was alive and in good health; and all of us rented
a van together to explore old haunts (including the steep hill down
to the river on what used to be Yasha's farm and Nekhe's home,
down which Nekhe and I used to roll as small children). But when
it came to Niemież, which had now expanded to the size of a small
town, we drew a blank. Following some local children's directions
to where "the school" was, we came to a large modern building
that was clearly not it; it then occurred to us to ask for "the old
school," which again turned out to be a considerably younger
building than the one we were looking for, and therefore once

again not it. We finally concluded that the house that my grand-parents built was no longer in existence, and gave up the search.

But if many physical remains of my childhood were not to be found, I did, somewhat unexpectedly, discover the actual facts of what took place on that fateful day in June of 1941, when Yasha, Velvl, and Velvl's two children—the teenage boy (now deceased) named Khayim–Dovid, and the adolescent daughter (now a grandmother) named Nekhe—had packed a wagon high with belongings, harnessed the two best horses, and headed east. Now, fifty-five years later, as we sat in Nekhe's apartment over hot tea served in glasses with metal holders, dipping into a wonderful homemade concoction of freshly picked wild mushrooms in sour cream sauce and conversing in the juicy Vilna Yiddish that I knew so well, Nekhe told us the true story of that day. As they were passing through Niemież racing eastward, knowing that the German armored divisions were only a day or so behind them (so she recounted), her father pulled up the horses and said: "Yasha, go quickly and take leave of your mother. We can spare the few minutes." But Yasha replied: "I can't do that. If I try to say good-bye, I will immediately begin to plead with her to come with us, and she will refuse. And then I, too, will stay. Drive on."

"So that was it," I remember thinking; but it was not until considerably later that I truly recognized what had taken place.

Because, while it is a frequently held opinion that God wants nothing else of us but to wait for and follow orders, I believe that (as is true for any other good parent) God's greatest pleasure comes from our embracing the duty of growing up—not, of course, by shedding our limitations and becoming divine, but by being aware of our limitations and acting responsibly within them. And at that moment, with the two horses pawing impatiently at the pavement, Yasha did just that. Aware of his own limitations—limitations that were, after all, profoundly human—he made an emotionally wrenching decision that, he recognized, was the best choice both for his mother and for him; and, in spite of the pain involved, he was able to muster the immense strength to act on it.

That is the gift of the incarnation.

7 ❧ RELIGION

When I was four years old, my older brother Uriel is once supposed to have remarked to my parents, "I'm very much afraid that Gabi is becoming religious." That's the way I heard it from my mother years later. She was highly amused, but unfortunately never gave me any explanation for what might have led six-year-old Uriel to put forward such a hypothesis. The question is complicated by a paradox that governed my family's life throughout my childhood, namely that while we regarded the Jewish religion with profound admiration and respect, we made no pretense whatsoever of believing any of it even one little bit. I was reminded of this as an adult when a good friend who had begun life as a "cradle Episcopalian" but found herself drifting away from it as she got older once cut off a conversation with me by saying "There's one thing about religion: either you believe in God, or you don't." What she meant, of course, was that belief in God functions as the very center, the keystone so to speak, of religion; and that if ever this primary belief begins to weaken, the rest will necessarily disintegrate—just as an architectural arch will collapse when the keystone is removed. But logical as this point of view may appear at first glance, I don't believe that it is necessarily correct; and much of my history illustrates this.

The truth is that all my life I have experienced a certain interest in and even longing toward what one might call, for lack of a better phrase, "religious things." When, at the age of eight or so, I first read the creation chapters of Yehoash's Yiddish translation of Genesis (at my own initiative; the book was, of course, around the house, but no one had particularly suggested that I read it), I immediately decided that I would write my own scroll of the creation of the world, and even enlisted Uriel's collaboration. We used a roll of kitchen parchment paper, and I illuminated the initial letter of every chapter in watercolor, showing the sun, the moon, and other details of creation. Unfortunately I don't remember anything about the content of our text, except that the name of the creator God was Abra.

All this took place against the background of a household that was strictly atheist: not only was there no thought of attending synagogue, we never even had a passover *seder* meal, which for many Jewish families functions as a last vestige of religious practice that continues to hold on long after every other type of observance has been abandoned. My father never wore a hat, and we not only mixed meat with dairy at our meals but ate pork freely (and even shellfish when it was available). Any suggestion that this may, in some sense, not be "right" would have been considered preposterous: why abandon the gifts of modern progress?

After the family settled in New York in 1941 our basic practice did not change, but there was a subtle shift in attitude. This was due to the fact that the war was raging in Europe and, as the months and years wore on, it was becoming clearer and clearer that not only were Jews being destroyed but *all* Jews were being destroyed—the middle-class Jews (like us) who had rejected religion as medieval superstition, and the poor Jews in the urban slums and rural *shtetl*[s] to whom faith was the breath of life. This realization led to a much mellower attitude on our part toward the various styles of Jewishness that had once existed but existed no longer. Some time soon after the war (perhaps in 1946, when I would have been eighteen), when the extent of the destruction of European Jewry was fully known, my father announced that we were going to celebrate a passover *seder* that year. "But who will read the haggadah?" I demanded. (The haggadah is the Hebrew liturgy that is recited at the seder.) "It's got to be read with the correct chant!" My father, who not only grew up in a somewhat assimilated setting but was completely tone-deaf to boot, freely admitted that he couldn't do it, and so he invited Mendl Elkin, the head librarian of the YIVO and a good friend, to officiate; Mr. Elkin, considerably older, had grown up in a traditionally religious household and had no problem with the chant. And so, thanks to my stubborn teenage insistence, it ended up being done "right."

That passover celebration was a memorable event, and became a tradition in our household that continued for years. On one of those occasions I even borrowed some recording equipment and recorded Mr. Elkin's recitation from beginning to end; then, for weeks afterwards, I sat in fascination and played it back over and over again, making elaborate musical notations. There was, I felt, something immeasurably precious in it, some fragment of an indefinable "real thing" that I, a microscopic David, needed to protect against the Goliath tidal wave of annihilation.

Yet in spite of the traditional melodies, in spite of all the males having their heads covered in orthodox fashion, in spite of the haggadah being read from cover to cover and not just *pro forma* as it often is, the fact remains that nobody around that table—not my father, not my mother, not Uriel or I or Mr. Elkin or any of the other guests—would have said that they believed in God. God was a medieval superstition. God was a hypothesis that science had made obsolete. God was a poetical expression of human longings, perhaps, but certainly no more than a metaphor.

My memory is unclear on how long those seders continued during my father's lifetime, but I do know that in 1970, a few months after his death, my mother felt the need to bring them back to life. By then Mr. Elkin had also been dead for a number of years, as was Uriel and all the other knowledgeable guests who had at one time graced our table, and my mother asked me whether I would be willing to officiate. This was, of course, on the face of it a preposterous idea: my background in respect to the haggadah consisted of bits and pieces that had seeped into my mind by osmosis over the years, covered over by an inchoate sauce of misty memories of Mr. Elkin's chant. My ability to sight-read Hebrew rapidly enough to keep up with the style was, to say the least, questionable. (I would have had no problem with Yiddish, but Hebrew, although it uses the same alphabet, is harder because only consonants are written as letters, the vowels being indicated sporadically by tiny symbols above and below.)

I could be cynical and say that I consented to my mother's request in the knowledge that the others at the table would be even more ignorant than I, giving me an opportunity to fake it and even earn some admiration for my supposed "proficiency," but that would not be quite fair. Granted that the urge to show off was there, much more important in my heart was a conviction that, to misquote a popular proverb, "Anything worth doing is worth doing badly." I knew that my own Jewish world was, like my father and my brother, dead, and that I was powerless to bring it back; and I felt called to pay it my last respects in the best way I knew how, helpless and fragmentary though it had to be. And if truth be told, I doubt very much that I was fooling anybody at that table; rather, they were grateful for my clumsy attempt because, at heart, they all felt exactly the same as I.

A few years later, after I had married Gerane and got in the habit of occasionally accompanying her to church, I met Gordon Jones, at that time the rector of Saint Andrew's Episcopal Church in Ann Arbor. He was a learned man whom I respected and liked, and I enjoyed conversing with him about various "religious" subjects such as Bible, church history and history in general (including Jewish history), and what various philosophers had to say about this or that; and I will never forget how, in the middle of one of those conversations, the startling realization suddenly came upon me that, when Gordon used the word "God," what he meant was—God! This discovery absolutely stunned me. Of course I used that word too, in phrases like "God willing," "God forbid," "for God's sake," and "Oh my God"; but I had always assumed that no person capable of intelligent thought could mean anything literal by it, anything based on any notion that an entity called "God" might actually exist. But the curious thing was that, having made that discovery, I also discovered that (at that moment in my life) it really didn't make a whole lot of difference. I felt no need to stop the conversation and say, "Excuse me, Gordon, but there's been a misunderstanding: when you say 'God,' you apparently mean 'God'; but when I say 'God,' I mean . . . well, it's hard to explain. I'm not sure what I mean."

Thinking about it now, my mind goes back to the creation scroll that Uriel and I put together when we were children. Had I then been asked whether I really believed in God, my answer would have been "No, of course not" because—though I had little real inkling of what the question meant—I knew "No" to be the "correct" answer, the answer that the adults around me would have given. But my eight-year-old excitement over the scroll, and its recounting of Abra's mighty works, had nothing to do with the strictly intellectual question of God's existence. Rather, it had its origin in what I *experienced* when I originally read the biblical account of creation. There was a certain otherworldly elegance about that account; I was impressed, I think, by the overall cadence and meter, by the authority with which it spoke, and by the fact that almost every sentence began with the word *and.* (This is a feature of the Hebrew narrative style that some older English translations also maintain, as does Yehoash's Yiddish.) At that age I probably already knew that the actual reason for the alternation of days and nights is connected with the spherical earth spinning about its axis, nor did I have any doubt of the correctness of that explanation (as I still don't); but how exciting, how powerful, to be suddenly confronted with a completely different view of the same truth! At that time I would not have known the word, but what I was experiencing—perhaps for the first time, certainly not the last—was a sense of *grandeur;* and I wanted to plug into that grandeur, by writing a creation scroll of my own.

That episode tells us a great deal of what religion is about. It always begins, I think, with a sensitivity to grandeur, which at one time or another everyone experiences: the grandeur of a sunset, the grandeur of a driving sea, the grandeur of a magnificent poem, the grandeur of a life well lived. But my reaction upon first reading Yehoash's Genesis went further than that in two important ways: first, it was not passive, but called for *activity* (I suddenly felt the need to write a creation scroll of my own); second, it was not solitary, but called for *community* (it was important for me to get Uriel to join me in the project). To my mind, *an active response to grandeur that depends upon community* is the essential meaning of religion.

Whether or not careful scrutiny would reveal weaknesses in this definition is, to me, less important than the general observation that, contrary to the opinion of the friend whom I quoted earlier in the chapter, *religion does not necessarily begin with God.* Indeed, I don't think anybody ever embraced religion on the basis of a purely logical proof of God's existence, because I don't believe that such a proof exists; that is, many proofs exist, but none that is convincing to a nonbeliever. (Conversely, of course, there is no proof of God's nonexistence either—that is, none that is convincing to a believer.) Religion is, in other words, not at all the same as faith, which in my case did not come until much later.

Most people I go to church with today may have difficulty identifying with such a view. That's because most people I go to church with grew up in families where religion already played a more or less "legitimate" and established role. To attend services on Sundays, perhaps to say grace before family meals, and to use the word "God" in connection with matters of morality was considered "normal." Children growing up in such a context know that the correct answer to "Do you believe in God?" is "Yes," just as I knew that it was "No." I, by contrast, can remember only one incident in my whole childhood of setting foot in any kind of house of worship, and that was on a school field trip to the magnificent Great Synagogue of Vilna—not, of course, while a service was in progress. Some years later, when I was a teenager in New York, a bunch of us, out on the town on Christmas Eve, decided to make a stop at Saint Patrick's Cathedral and take in a piece of the midnight mass. We stood respectfully at the back of the nave and watched as, what seemed an enormous distance away, people in strange and colorful costumes were executing a strange and colorful pantomime. (In those days the liturgy was still in Latin, and so would not have been broadcast over the public-address system. The only sound would have been that of the occasional sanctus bell—plus, of course, the music.) After some minutes, we shrugged our shoulders and went back out into the snow. But the first time in my life that I attended a real live synagogue service was not until one Yom Kippur when I was already an Episcopal priest.

But if the experience with the Abra scroll at the age of eight constituted my first personal encounter with religion, my attitude toward our family's first passover seder, a decade later and many thousands of miles away, revealed a further elaboration: my insistence that the haggadah be read from beginning to end, and with a "correct" (that is, traditional) chant. Seeing that my background included no experience with Jewish worship, the enormous urge to do it that way is nothing if not surprising. Yet I was apparently aware that, in order for religion to work, the community that is so central to it must be experienced as continuous not merely in space but also in time. There is no such thing as a "religion of the moment": it must be done "the way it has always been done"—or at least feel like it is.

Fifty-five years later, I can see clearly how paradoxical those feelings were. After all, Jewish religion in America is hardly dead. Had I been looking for a Jewish religious community to join, I would have had a large choice of congregations, ranging from *Reform* (where religious practice is to a large degree modernized), through *Conservative* (where the liturgy is more or less traditional, but members are fairly autonomous in how they conduct their private lives), to assorted gradations of *Orthodox*, and finally all the way to fundamentalist groups who refuse to deviate one iota from the way their ancestors lived in Europe two and three hundred years ago. My yearning, however, was not for any of those, but for a religious way of celebrating my family's former life, *which was, of course, not religious.* And since that former life's continuity in time had been amputated by events of the Second World War, I unconsciously grafted on to it a different continuity, one that led back to a style of Jewish religious observance of which my family, at least in recent generations, had never been a part. And here it is worth noting that, whereas the idea of having a family seder in the first place had definitely originated with my father, what he had had in mind was, I believe, a simple—if poignant—symbolic expression of solidarity with victims of the Holocaust. By contrast, it was I who felt driven to insist on the full integrity of the liturgy, that is, on making our meal into a *correct* religious observance, done "the way it has always been done" (even though it was not at all the way *we* had ever done it). By the same token it was I, officiating at those few last seders at my mother's house as the blind leading the blind, who knew in my heart that it was all over.

"I'm very much afraid," Uriel had said when I was four, "that Gabi is becoming religious." Perhaps his insight was more profound than anyone at the time appreciated.

On April 8, 1971, a day before leaving for New York to officiate at what would turn out to be the last of my mother's seders, I met Gerane on a blind date, and we were married on October 23 of that year, thus merging our two families. Among the things we found out about each other on that first date was that Gerane was an Episcopalian who regularly attended Saint Andrew's Church, whereas Gabi was a Jew without religion (I did not, at that time, share Uriel's childhood intuition). Neither one of us had any particular problem with that. Every Sunday, Gerane and little Natalie, who was then four, got dressed up and took off for church, and the rest of us (including Gerane's teenage children) did whatever one does on a lazy Sunday morning. This routine continued smoothly until the end of March, when Gerane told me that Good Friday was approaching, and that she would go to church alone because it is a grief-filled occasion that she has trouble explaining to children. I volunteered to accompany her, partly out of the simple solidarity of love, but perhaps also because grief was something I felt familiar with. The quiet church was impressive with its stained–glass windows and dark oak paneling, devoid of any trace of decoration except the somber black veil covering the cross, and the long silences of the service were punctuated by words that were calm, clear, and comprehensible. There was no music. "These people," was the thought that passed through my mind, "know what they are doing because it is the way they have always done it. Clearly, this is a place where religion lives."

A year later, I again accompanied Gerane on Good Friday in what we playfully felt had become an annual tradition. This time, however, as I was listening to the words and silences of the service, Gerane whispered to me that it would all look very different two days later; I was struck with curiosity and decided to return. The contrast was, of course, stunning. The church was brimming over with flowers, its pews filled by smiling people decked out in festive Easter pastels. At ten o'clock precisely, a stirring brass fanfare shook the rafters, followed immediately by the sound of the organ filling the huge space. As the congregation rose to its feet and broke into the opening hymn, the procession appeared: crucifer and cross; acolytes with torches; the fully vested choir; and finally, bringing up the rear, the priests in white and gold. When the procession reached the altar, the music stopped, and I began to hear the measured cadences of Elizabethan English of the service itself, it absolutely took my breath away.

Now it may be said—and it would be perfectly true—that by witnessing the transition from Good Friday to Easter Sunday I entered Christianity through the front door; but on a conscious level, at least, I experienced nothing that theologically definable. Faith was, for me, still in the distant future. What I did sense, however, and quite distinctly at that, is that here, at Saint Andrew's Episcopal Church on Easter morning, listening to the words and music that joyously proclaimed Christ's resurrection, I was suddenly standing in the presence of Abra himself, the great and ancient God of Religion, now newly risen from the dead.

8 ❧ BAPTISM

Since baptism is the formal step that officially makes one into a Christian, this chapter might well have been the last one had this book been concerned only with formal and official steps. For reasons that the Prologue already made clear, however, it will merely conclude the book's first half.

By way of introduction: if one regards "Judaism" and "Christianity" simply as the names of two religions, one of the striking ways in which those religions differ is in the manner in which membership in them is attained. As we pointed out in a previous chapter, one becomes a Christian by being individually *baptized*, a ritual procedure that requires being sprinkled with (or, in some traditions, immersed in) water with the uttering of a trinitarian formula—that is, "In the name of the Father, and of the Son, and of the Holy Spirit." By contrast, Judaism requires, in the overwhelming number of cases, no procedure at all: one is automatically a Jew by virtue of being born into a Jewish family. This difference underlines how the beginning of Judaism, like the beginning of the chicken–and–egg cycle, is totally lost in prehistory: you cannot become a Jew by birth unless there were Jews who preceded you. Indeed, Jews entered history as an already formed *tribe*, sharing not only what we today call religion but also ethnicity, language, culture, customs, the understanding of one's past, the understanding of one's place in the world, and everything else that makes up the life of a society. Modern discussions of whether Jews are "really" a religion, or "really" an ethnic group, or "really" a linguistic unit, or "really" a cultural unit, and so forth generally founder because of a lack of understanding of the way in which Jews are all of the above.

The situation is radically different with regard to Christianity: far from having its origins buried in the prehistoric past, the exact details of how it originated are, to church–going Christians, the object of intense attention. According to the writings of the New Testament (which in this case there is no reason to doubt), Jesus of Nazareth was a Jew, as were the audiences to whom he preached and the disciples that he called. As to whether he was also technically a Christian, opinions can differ: the Gospels testify that he was baptized by John the Baptist in the river Jordan, but there is no mention of a trinitarian formula; on the other hand, it is said that at that moment the Holy Spirit descended upon him in the form of a dove, which could be considered an adequate equivalent. Obviously, though, the whole question is a bit silly. Even though there are no reports of either Jesus or the first generation of disciples being baptized according to later literal standards, the last words that Jesus, after his resurrection, said to his followers were, according to Matthew's Gospel, "Go therefore and make disciples of all nations, baptizing them in the name of the Father, and of the Son, and of the Holy Spirit." Whether or not that report is itself accurate, this is exactly what his disciples and their successors have been doing ever since.

Interestingly, neither Judaism nor Christianity has any provision for *renouncing* the religion once one has become a member. With regard to Judaism, that is self-evident: there is no way of ceasing to have been born of Jewish parents. Therefore, whatever a Jew does—including having himself baptized—he does as a Jew, and remains a Jew afterwards. In terms of traditional Jewish values, that makes the acceptance of baptism a particularly heinous step. The Yiddish word *meshumed*, from the Hebrew for "one who has been obliterated," refers literally to a person who has taken that step, but metaphorically to any kind of what we would today describe as "repulsive lowlife," one who is beneath contempt. That is the millennia-old heritage of Judaism as a survival machine, which everyone who has grown up as a Jew carries in his or her blood.

Some of my Christian friends express puzzlement that such an intense sense of betrayal could attach to this act when, as in my case, a person's Jewishness was absolutely secular and no belief in God was involved. In fact, however, the perception of ultimate faithfulness, perhaps even martyrdom, as necessarily depending on God or religion is a misunderstanding; allegiance to a nation, or to a culture, or to a way of life, or even to a language, can be equally powerful, as the various wars of nationalism of recent centuries have demonstrated. Remember that originally Judaism was everything that befits a tribe, including (but not limited to) religion. When in the middle of the nineteenth century the birth of secular Judaism had the consequence, for people who embraced it, that religion was omitted from the list, that in no way removed—or even appreciably lessened—the fierce loyalty to what remained. And that is the heritage I brought with me when, having married Gerane in 1971, I began to attend Saint Andrew's Episcopal Church in Ann Arbor, and to be involved in its activities with ever greater regularity and intensity.

In those years, the principal Episcopal Sunday service alternated between "Morning Prayer," in which the people remain in their pews throughout; and "Holy Communion," in which at one point the members of the congregation go up to the altar and receive the bread and wine that signify Christ's body and blood. I had no problem with Morning Prayer; I just sat respectfully (except for the hymns, when I stood and sang with everyone else) and imagined myself as an interested but uninvolved visitor. But Communion was different; everybody except me filed up to the altar, then returned and knelt in silent meditation, while I felt lonely and sticking out like a sore thumb. Since I had not yet struck up my later cordial friendship with the rector, I prevailed upon Gerane to ask him privately "what would happen if, unbaptized, I wished to join in receiving communion," and he told her that, "according to the new rules," that would be just fine, and I would be cordially welcomed.

In fact that was a half-truth, given to us by a very wise priest. The full but somewhat complicated story was the following. The then current Book of Common Prayer contained a rubric at the end of the Confirmation Service that read *"And there shall none be admitted to the Holy Communion, until such time as he be confirmed, or be ready and desirous to be confirmed."* (Confirmation, of course, presupposes baptism.) During the late 1960s, however, a new era of lively discussion about liturgical reform (leading to the Book of Common Prayer of 1979, but in fact still continuing today) had begun, during which this rubric came under early and intense scrutiny for at least two reasons. First, the new ecumenical spirit of the times recoiled at the thought of limiting communion to Episcopalians, rather than welcoming Christians of all denominations. Second, there was an increasing feeling that communion ought not to be withheld from children, as indeed the Eastern Orthodox churches have never done. For these reasons, the General Convention of the Episcopal Church had in 1970 authorized a book of "Services for Trial Use," which contained, as its very first item, a new Service of Confirmation that lacked the old restrictive rubric, with the idea that from now on all Christians—Episcopalians or Methodists, children or adults—would be treated equally.

At the time, only a small group of unusually knowledgeable and perceptive people realized that, with the omission of that particular rubric, there remained in the whole Book of Common Prayer no restriction whatsoever on who may receive communion. This group did, however, number our rector among them, and that was the basis on which he gave us his ruling. On the other hand, it was not at all what General Convention had had in mind, and as the years passed apparently more and more people became unhappy over it. Finally, in 1985 (long after the new Book of Common Prayer had been fully approved) Convention acted again by passing a new canon—Title I, Canon 17, Section 7— which reads: *"No unbaptized person shall be eligible to receive Holy Communion in this Church."* This new canon had no bearing on me personally, however, since by then I had been baptized.

To me, the rector's dispensation opened a new universe. There was, of course, the sheer inner experience of receiving communion, which I will not attempt to express in words. More interesting in my specific case is my resulting odd perception that, whereas ordinarily baptism is required to make a person into a Christian, my own case was so exceptional that this requirement didn't apply. By some very special and unique phenomenon akin to virgin birth, I felt, I have been personally exempted, becoming a full-fledged Christian without needing to take the step which, I knew in my Jewish blood, would turn me into repulsive lowlife beneath contempt. I am that ultimate and unique exception, at the same time both Jew and Christian, both Christian and Jew. Of course most of my friends and acquaintances in the parish, seeing me at the communion rail regularly, had no idea of the complexity of my status and assumed that I was baptized.

I don't know exactly what the rector's thoughts were at the time, but his pastoral gut feeling, namely that my idiosyncratic view of my own Christianity is one that he should neither explicitly support nor explicitly shoot down, was (in my present opinion) superb. Only once did he express some uneasiness, saying that my increasing involvement at Saint Andrew's was bound to lead someone, sooner or later, to nominate me for vestry (the governing board of the parish), on which I couldn't serve because I was really not a Christian and so, strictly speaking, not a member of the church. Personally, I felt that it would be no problem; we (the rector and I) could simply explain that being unbaptized made no difference in my special case; but he didn't see it that way. On this point, he said, the canons are unequivocal. If truth be told, at the time I felt a bit miffed by his unwillingness to put my specialness above a silly bunch of canons, but my respect and love for him prevailed.

This situation lasted until 1981 when, having served Saint Andrew's for twenty years, the rector retired. By then, my stature in the parish was firmly established. Among other things, I offered a regular Bible study program entitled "Month of Sundays," which met in the evening of the first Sunday of each month to consider the Bible readings that would be coming up during the month to follow. In the summer of 1982 I also became the first coordinator of the newly established Saint Andrew's Breakfast Program, which offered a free breakfast six days a week to anyone who wanted it; this entailed a lot of work, since a large number of volunteers were involved. Yet with the old rector gone there was no one left to support my peculiar status with regard to baptism, a matter which acquired a particular urgency because there was now serious talk of having me run for vestry at the next annual parish meeting in January.

On the other hand, accepting baptism, which I now knew would be required to serve on vestry, meant not only giving up my private "specialness" and miserably betraying the Jewishness which—some would say paradoxically—had become much more precious to me since I discovered my Christian affinity; in addition, I felt that it would be doubly wrong to undergo baptism *as a means to something else.* The same contempt that I have always felt for Jews who take that step to land a better job, or a better house, or a better marriage, or even (perhaps) because it would save them from being killed in a pogrom, I must now feel equally for a Jew who does it in order to be on the vestry of Saint Andrew's Church. Baptism must be accepted for the sake of baptism, for the sake of being a Christian, or not at all. Therefore, the question I put to myself is this: suppose I go through baptism, then put myself up as a candidate for vestry at the annual meeting *and lose.* What would be my reaction? Would it be "What a waste, I made myself into a piece of repulsive lowlife, and all for nothing"? Or would it be "Too bad about the election, but the wonderful thing is that I am now a real Christian, and it makes me glad"?

Did I really, deep in my heart, want to be baptized?

Emphatically yes. My life as a Christian was already full of joy and challenge, consistently fascinating and consistently surprising. It brought me not only the satisfaction of exploring an intellectual world that was at the same time very new and very old but, I already sensed, it had the capacity in some mysterious way of bringing out the best in me as a human being. As for the element of betrayal, I decided there really wasn't any. The Jewish culture with which I grew up, and which meant so much to me, is in any case dead and gone; indeed, I personally felt more profoundly Jewish after a few years of pursuing my religious interests at Saint Andrew's than I had ever done before in my adult life. Rather than giving anything up, I can literally keep my Judaism and, by baptism, be a Christian too. And so I made up my mind.

Although the fashion had by then shifted to baptisms performed as part of a principal Sunday service in front of the whole congregation, I preferred to have mine small and private, with only the sponsors (or "Godparents") present; this required the approval of the new rector (who, at this point, had already arrived), who started out skeptical but at length relented. The officiating priest was a good friend of mine, a woman whom the old rector had hired as an assistant and who had been acting as rector during the "interregnum"; and the sponsors I had chosen were Gerane, the retired rector (who fulfilled the role *in absentia* since he had already moved away from Ann Arbor), the new rector, and two treasured friends from the parish.

As to the question of whether my motivation had, deep down, been merely a desire to run for vestry—especially since the parish's already soured relationship with the new rector was heating up and I was seen by many as the perfect vestryman to stand up to him—I remembered from my childhood a story that was told about Napoleon, who was something of a folk hero to Eastern European Jews (probably because his French soldiers, who passed through the region early in the nineteenth century, were not characterized by the savage and violent antisemitism that was automatically expected of local armies). The folk tales about him all featured Napoleon's austere lifestyle and granite will, as illustrated, for example, by his habit of always sleeping on a simple iron army cot; and the particular one that came back to me now had Napoleon waking in the middle of a cold night with a powerful craving for a pinch of snuff. Knowing that his snuffbox was on the dresser on the other side of the room, he was faced with a dilemma: to yield to such a craving for luxury would demonstrate a lack of willpower, but to ignore it might raise the suspicion that he was too soft to leave his warm bed. Under the circumstances, Napoleon did the only possible thing: he got out from under his cozy blanket, crossed the room barefoot on the freezing floor, *but did not take any snuff* before returning to bed.

The following Sunday, following Napoleon's example, I told all my friends and supporters that I was withdrawing my candidacy for vestry; and soon after that Gerane and I transferred our membership from Saint Andrew's to Saint Clare's.

INTERLUDE

9 ❧ JOURNEYS

FIRST JOURNEY

The Lord said to Abram, "Go from your country and your kindred and your

father's house to the land that I will show you. And I will make of you a

great nation, and I will bless you, and make your name great, so that you

will be a blessing. I will bless those who bless you, and him who curses you

I will curse; and by you all the families of the earth shall bless themselves."

My father was born in 1894 in Goldingen, a small town in Courland, which today is part of Latvia. In the Middle Ages, Courland was an important naval power on the Baltic Sea; around the year 1200 it came under the domination of the Order of Teutonic Knights, a domination that lasted until the sixteenth century when the Order was dissolved. This period nonetheless left its indirect mark in a prominence of the German language among Courland's gentry and intelligentsia (Latvian being the language of the peasants), and in the fact that today a majority of the population of Latvia is Lutheran (whereas neighboring Lithuania is overwhelmingly Roman Catholic). When my father was born there Courland was a province of the Russian empire, so its official state language was Russian; but when the independent nation of Latvia was created after the First World War, Latvian became the official language, and Goldingen became known by its Latvian name *Kuldiga*.

I doubt that this little town could, during my father's childhood, boast any paved streets or sidewalks, any running water, or any means of disposing of sewage other than street gutters. I have a vague memory of a studio photograph of my father's parents that stood on his desk when I was a child, but know little about that grandfather except that he owned a hardware store and died well before I was born. I did know my father's mother, however; she was very old, very sweet, and lived (by the time I knew her) in Riga, the capital of Latvia. Uriel and I were taught to address her as *Grossmama* (German for "grandma") because she spoke German, which was also my father's native tongue, but we pronounced the word with a Yiddish "o" which is much shorter than the German vowel. Being four or five years old at the time, I did not find it the least bit remarkable that my father spoke to his mother in a foreign language, nor do I remember having any difficulty communicating with her myself on the fairly rare occasions when we saw each other. Most likely she did, in fact, know Yiddish quite well from her own childhood; she was born in 1854, when Jews in Goldingen surely spoke Yiddish (as did most Jews in the rest of Eastern Europe). By the time their children were born, however, my paternal grandparents had apparently become free-thinking enough to go over in their day-to-day life to German, the language spoken by cultured gentiles around them; this is indicated by the fact that all ten children (of whom my father was the youngest) were given decidedly German names (his was Max). In addition, the same picture that stood on my father's desk showed *Grosspapa* (as he was referred to) completely bald without any kind of head covering, which definitely identifies him as having broken away from traditional Jewish religious practice.

My father's early schooling consisted, at first, of an only slightly modernized *kheder*, in which little boys were taught rudiments of the Bible and the prayer book. As far as I can reconstruct it, my father found himself immediately chafing at the bit because the scope of learning was so narrow and its pace so slow. The alternative was a gentile school with the pretentious title of *"Gymnasium* (that is, secondary school) for the Nobility of Courland," which was, apparently, glad to accept Jews so long as they paid their tuition and endured a certain amount of antisemitic abuse. This my father was at first willing to do in return for access to some real learning, but after a while it became painfully clear to him that the quality of education that the nobility of Courland demanded for its children was also marginal at best. So at the age of fourteen my father quit school altogether and shook the dust of his little home town off his feet, traveling 250 miles to the acknowledged cultural center of Eastern European Jewry, universally known among Jews by the nickname "Jerusalem of Lithuania." Here, he figured, he would be free to do his studying at the pace that his mind demanded.

And so my father embraced Vilna as his adopted home, and Yiddish as his adopted language. This does not mean, of course, that after that he necessarily stayed put. In 1912 we find him in Saint Petersburg, independently passing the examinations for secondary school diploma, which entitled him to take courses at the university in philology and history. A few years later he traveled to Germany, studying first at the University of Berlin and later at the University of Marburg, where in 1923 he was awarded the degree of Doctor of Philosophy. Yet it is interesting that in the customary autobiographical sketch submitted with his dissertation, where my father lists Goldingen as the place where he was born, he nonetheless refers to Vilna as his *Heimatstadt* or, literally, "native city."

When in 1925 my father returned to Vilna "for good," his first act was, in collaboration with two colleagues, to found the YIVO Institute. The name YIVO is an acronym for a Yiddish phrase that, translated, means "Jewish Institute of [Social] Science." It arose as the brainchild of a number of Jewish intellectuals who had come to the conclusion that if Eastern European Jews were to have access to the kind of secular higher education that could make them into modern research scholars (and so, in their view, bring the community into the twentieth century) it would have to be through quasi-academic institutions that they themselves founded.

My father, in particular, was a great admirer of the German system of universities that he had attended. Although well aware that (both in Berlin and in Marburg) antisemitism was hardly a rarity, he nonetheless saw it as a relic of the past that the future would surely eradicate. Unlike Saint Petersburg (and, for that matter, the rest of Russia), where Jew-hating was endemic and the government far too corrupt to fight it and far too bigoted to *want* to fight it, educated Germans—the people who understood the importance of card catalogs being accurate and meetings starting on time—could be depended on to respect true modern scholarship, of the type fostered by the great universities, wherever it originated. Jews in Vilna, now an important provincial city in the newly independent Polish Republic, were capable of establishing for themselves a similar modern standard of higher learning even if the still antisemitic government did not allow Jewish institutions to grant advanced degrees.

On October 26, 1929, the cornerstone of the YIVO building was laid. Ten years later, at the outbreak of the Second World War, it was not only the seat of a number of successful graduate programs on every subject of social science concerning Jews, but could boast a library of approximately one hundred thousand volumes and a document archive containing a comparable number of items. Jewish academia was on its way.

SECOND JOURNEY

Thus says the Lord, who makes a way in the sea, a path in the mighty waters, who brings forth chariot and horse, army and warrior; they lie down, they cannot rise, they are extinguished, quenched like a wick: "Remember not the former things, nor consider things of old. Behold, I am doing a new thing; now it springs forth, do you not perceive it?"

At the end of December 1940 Vladivostok, Russia's small window directly onto the Sea of Japan and indirectly onto the Pacific Ocean, was not a particularly elegant port: in the winter weather, its network of quays littered with dirty barrels and crates and ropes of all sizes seemed as colorless as a worn black–and–white photograph. But to a twelve–year–old boy like me, whose experience with seagoing ships was limited to what he had read in Jules Verne, it all presented an absolutely marvelous spectacle, especially when the bus that carried us from the hotel pulled up alongside the *Amakusa Maru,* which, I knew, would serve as our home for the next several days.

It was a long way from Vilna, which my mother and I had left on December 17, 1940. My father and Uriel were already settled in New York. They had sailed there from Copenhagen with a so–called "academic visa" that exempted them from American immigration quotas; subsequently, my father had been able to arrange for the American consulate in Moscow to issue a similar visa for my mother and me as his dependents. The problem was that we had no document in which the visa (which is basically a rubber stamp countersigned by the consul) could be placed: my mother's passport, which also included me as a dependent child, was a Polish one, and Poland as a nation no longer existed. Consequently, the first leg of our journey—from Vilna to Moscow—had to be done without any identity documents whatsoever. Once we reached Moscow, our visa was duly issued on a piece of paper furnished by the consulate, carrying the seal of the United States of America and therefore appropriately impressive–looking but itself signifying nothing.

Accordingly, our whole trip was highly irregular, depending for its success, first, on not attracting any attention; and second, on there not being anyone in Vilna who wanted to make trouble by reporting us to the authorities. We relied on Russian being my mother's native tongue, plus the fact that she had lived in Moscow as a teenager during the First World War and was therefore familiar with the city, to satisfy the first requirement (especially if I kept my mouth shut), but the second was more complex since there was no shortage of Communist political causes that my father had, over the years, offended. That's why we generally kept our departure a secret, pretending that we were going to visit our cousins in Kaunas for a week; but in fact we boarded the train heading back from Kaunas in the direction of Moscow the following morning. Of course we knew that there would be a twenty-minute stopover in Vilna and that someone on the station platform might easily recognize us, but we managed to spend those twenty minutes with our compartment door locked and the curtains tightly drawn, holding our breath until the train was safely in motion again. For me, and I suppose for my mother even more so, this was a strangely disturbing experience: to be sitting on a stopped train in the city that more than anything else represented reality for us, and to need to be hiding from that reality in a locked train compartment.

Yet we arrived in Moscow without incident, and the following day's business at the American consulate went smoothly as well; but since we were still without citizenship we would be in danger as long as we remained on Soviet soil. For this reason, we began the next leg of our journey without delay.

The nine-day trip on the Trans–Siberian Railway (today it only takes four days) covers a distance of close to six thousand miles and spans eight time zones in the process. Computing an average speed from the total distance and total time, one obtains approximately twenty-five miles per hour. It would be a mistake, however, to imagine that we were plodding along for nine days at that constant rate; as I recall it, we spent most of the time just standing still, sometimes at a station, other times in the middle of nowhere. We made the trip in an ordinary third–class carriage, which meant compartments with hard wooden benches. Fortunately, the train was not full (who, except for crazy people like us, would travel the Trans-Siberian in the dead of winter?), so that my mother and I could stretch out much of the time. Hard wooden benches are not particularly comfortable to sleep on, but twelve-year-old boys are adaptable. I imagine that my mother, who was forty-two, maintained a much more vivid memory of those conditions.

My main recollection of that trip, staring out the window, is of a vast, gray, and unchanging snow-covered landscape, just as one would imagine Siberia to be. To someone like my mother whose schooling included Russian geography, the names of the stations started out by being familiar: Sverdlovsk; Omsk; Novosibirsk; Krasnoyarsk; Irkutsk. After some days, however, it all turned into fairy land: Ulan-Ude, a seventeenth-century Cossak fortress; Birobidzhan, the center of the Soviet Autonomous Region that in 1928 had been allocated for a Jewish settlement, and whose rail station still carried its inscriptions both in Russian and Yiddish. But at length we did arrive in Vladivostok and had our first good night's sleep in a real, if modest, hotel.

The *Amakusa Maru*, which we boarded the next day, was a small vessel of about 2,300 tons displacement, which at that time plied the Sea of Japan between Vladivostok and the little Japanese port of Tsuruga in Fukui Prefecture. The crew consisted of very short people with high cheekbones who moved quickly, spoke a thoroughly incomprehensible language, and expressed their general friendliness by smiling a great deal. There were no cabins, just large open spaces below deck covered with bamboo mats on which one was not to walk without first removing one's shoes. The food was not interesting but plentiful: mostly steamed white rice with unfamiliar vegetables, to be eaten with little wooden sticks.

Soon we were ready to cast off. I watched in fascination as the Japanese crew, calling to each other in their enigmatic tongue, performed the intricate ballet that caused us to leave the quay behind and head out to sea. At the outer breakwater the ship slowed and the crowd of passengers that had collected at the starboard bow, I among them, watched as a ladder was thrown over the side and the Russian harbor pilot climbed down into a waiting launch, which immediately gunned its engine and turned back toward land.

"Now we are really and truly free," I heard my mother quietly say just behind me, her voice on the point of breaking. Surprised by her presence, I turned around and looked at her in puzzlement. Although I could hardly have been unaware of the radical changes that had taken place in our lives during the preceding sixteen months of wartime, the only people to be really feared—this I knew—were Hitler and the Germans; and they had now been stopped, thanks to brilliant Soviet diplomacy, a safe distance away. Comrade Stalin, on the other hand, was a wonderful man who loved not only workers and peasants but also children and flowers—that's what we had been taught in school. (At the time I was unaware that most of my teachers believed none of it themselves.) If we were traveling to America now, it was only because Papa and Uriel had been trapped in Copenhagen and not allowed back home because of stupid red tape. Yes, that's what I thought, and that's what my mother and grandmother wanted me to think, because the truth was too big for an adolescent boy who, in spite of his best intentions, could so easily betray us all. It was an indication of the supreme trust that I had in the adults of the family that all the terrible charades with which I had had to play along did not basically shake my faith that everything was all right with the world. Now I briefly considered asking my mother what she had meant by her odd remark, but decided to leave it for another day.

We docked in Tsuruga after two days at sea and immediately got on a night train to Kobe, a major seaport on the Pacific coast of Japan. Here we were scheduled to wait approximately four weeks for the ship that would take us to the United States. As it happened, however, we did not wait nearly that long: the *President Pierce*, due to sail for San Francisco in a mere eight days, had just had a cancellation for two berths, which my mother instantly grabbed. In view of the unpredictability of wartime, I think she was wise. In fact, it would turn out that we were only months away from the Japanese attack on Pearl Harbor, which would have left us stranded, stateless, penniless, and probably interned in Japan.

Unlike the *Amakusa Maru*, the American ship *President Pierce* was a full-size ocean-going passenger vessel, of about 22,000 tons displacement and 535 feet in length. It sailed from Kobe on January 8, 1941, and, after a stopover in Honolulu, arrived in San Francisco on January 28, from where a five-day transcontinental train trip brought us to New York and reunion with my father and Uriel.

It is interesting how much my mother and I, after ten days of immersion in Japanese surroundings, felt instantly at home when we boarded the *President Pierce*. It was not just being surrounded by people who "looked normal" and ate familiar-looking fare sitting at tables using forks and knives; but that, in spite of neither of us knowing a word of English, we found communication with fellow passengers and crew infinitely more straightforward. The familiar alphabet, and the consequent recognizability of written cognate words, played an important role in this, as did the fact that it was never difficult to find someone who could translate between English and either German, Polish, Yiddish, or Russian, all of which languages were accessible to us.

THIRD JOURNEY

Then Samson called to the Lord and said, "O Lord God, remember me, I pray thee, and strengthen me, I pray thee, only this once, O God, that I may be avenged upon the Philistines for one of my two eyes." And Samson grasped the two middle pillars upon which the building rested, and he leaned his weight upon them, his right hand on the one and his left hand on the other. And Samson said, "Let me die with the Philistines." Then he bowed with all his might; and the building fell down upon the lords and upon all the people who were in it. So the dead whom he slew at his death were more than those whom he had slain during his life.

When my father and Uriel arrived in New York in March of 1940, the local YIVO branch, until then concerned mainly with raising funds for its parent institution in Vilna, was housed in a single room on the Lower East Side of Manhattan. Seven years later, with the Institute ensconced in a handsome building of its own on West

123rd Street, my father wrote to a close Vilna friend who had lived through the Holocaust and now resided in Paris: "I don't know how to explain to you that the YIVO in America is still fighting for recognition. . . . The worst thing is not that several million of the five million Jews [in the United States] don't understand any Yiddish . . . but that the ones that do understand it don't have a high opinion of the language and are not creative. . . . In which case, why have a YIVO at all? Psychologically one could perhaps say: out of stubbornness. . . . But there are [logical] reasons as well: without Yiddish, Jews are impoverished, . . . isolated from Jews of other lands and from [their] past."

In fact, my father's stubbornness (which he obviously acknowledges with a sense of pride) did pay off handsomely, but not exactly in the way he envisaged in 1947. If today the YIVO is known and respected by anyone interested in Jewish history or Jewish social science it is because, under my father's direction, it essentially jettisoned the dwindling clientele of older Yiddish-speakers and addressed itself more and more to young Jews who knew essentially nothing of the language other than what they remembered from their uneducated grandparents or learned in YIVO courses or in various college and university programs that the YIVO inspired.

Two factors kept my father going in this endeavor. The first was that, at the end of the war, it turned out that large segments of the YIVO's Vilna library and archives had survived—partly thanks to friends on the scene who risked, and often sacrificed, their lives to conceal important materials so they could be salvaged after the war by those who knew the secret hiding places (including a number of people who fled the Vilna ghetto before its liquidation in 1943 to join the partisans); and partly because the Germans themselves shipped a lot of stuff off to Germany for the purpose of starting a museum about Jews when the subjects themselves were no longer in existence. Most of those documents, largely due to my father's obstinate energy, ended up in the New York YIVO's possession during the late 1940s.

On the basis of those materials, my father in 1946 wrote his first postwar book: *Hitler's Professors: The Part of Scholarship in Germany's Crimes against the Jewish People.* The book is a meticulously documented

account of the essentially unanimous way in which German scholars cooperated in what we today call the Holocaust, that is, Hitler's
plan to provide the "final solution to the Jewish question" by erad-
icating all Jews. To my father, however, *Hitler's Professors* was also a
very personal response to what he perceived as a very personal betrayal. Twenty-five years earlier he had, after all, admired German
scholarship as a paradigm of an intellectual culture that, in many
ways, he wanted to emulate; is it any wonder that he found these
revelations so terribly shattering? While no Jew, knowing the essential facts of the Holocaust, could have felt particularly friendly
toward Germans, in my father's case the absolute hatred of Germans
became an obsession. He spoke little of it, but in my mind's eye I
can imagine him sitting up in bed in the middle of the night, his
heart pounding, while he stares into the darkness with but one
thought in mind—how he hates the Germans.

As a result of those feelings, he also vowed to stop using the
German language altogether, either in speaking or in writing, re-
sponding to German correspondence either in Yiddish—when it
seemed reasonable to suppose that the other party understood it
—or in English.

The second factor that kept my father going was Uriel. My
brother Uriel was two years older than I and, even as a child,
showed a passion for linguistics (just as I showed a passion for
science and technology). Although I can by no means complain
that my father neglected me—he was, in every way, a devoted and
loving parent—the fact that Uriel shared his interest gave the two
of them a natural closeness that I did not share. And as Uriel grew
in age, so he grew in wisdom and accomplishment, inducing my
father to write to a friend that Uriel's linguistic work was characterized by "Vilna standards." This was a great understatement: had
Uriel done the same work in Vilna, he would still have been
viewed as exceptionally talented.

In 1952 a wealthy admirer offered to endow, expressly for my
father, a special chair of Yiddish Language, Literature, and Culture
at Columbia University, hoping to relieve him of administrative
YIVO duties so that he could engage fully in scholarly work. Over
the protest of many good friends (including me), he declined, feel-

ing that he simply could not abandon his duties at the YIVO. However, he told his would-be benefactor that he did have a candidate to suggest, namely his son Uriel. Both the donor and the university demurred strongly, since Uriel had just barely received his PhD and had, at that time, absolutely no status (I believe he was an instructor in the linguistics department), so the thing smelled of simple nepotism. At my father's stubborn insistence, however, a compromise was arranged whereby the donor decreased the salary fraction of his gift substantially and the university agreed to give Uriel the unusual title of Assistant Professor on an Endowed Chair, with an assistant professor's salary and without tenure. It didn't take long, however, before Uriel's work in linguistics was widely known and admired, resulting in the general opinion that Columbia University had gotten quite a bargain in hiring him at that early stage. Tenure (and a proper salary) came a short time later.

My father's joy and pride at Uriel's success was understandable; any parent would share those feelings. But it seems to me that, for him, there was another element. After all, Max Weinreich, the obsessive perfectionist especially where Yiddish was involved, could not but be aware that the level of Yiddish at the YIVO was, slowly but surely, going downhill. Outstanding as the place was (and still is) in its library and archival collections covering every possible aspect of Jewish life, the people who work there, even if they are experts in their fields, do from time to time make mistakes in their Yiddish. I cannot, of course, hold it against them, since not many of them grew up in Vilna (or a similar center of vibrant Jewish culture) with Yiddish as their mother tongue; but errors that even I notice must have been a source of great pain to my father, signifying (as he probably saw it) his own failure to reproduce in New York the world of Vilna (or, as he had some years earlier written in a letter, "to *Vilnaize* New York").

Of course at the time of Uriel's initial successes my father must have already realized how impossible the task was that in 1940 he had set for himself: to replace not only an uprooted young tree (the Vilna YIVO had, after all, been only fifteen years old at the time of its destruction), but to reproduce the structure of the ground and soil in which it grew—which transformed it from a matter of horticulture to a matter of geology. But there *was* Uriel, who not only fully satisfied the standard of the Vilna YIVO but far exceeded it. My father's life had been, to be sure, one filled with sorrow and sacrifice, but with Uriel as an heir a man can hope to defeat even geological time.

Then, at the age of forty, Uriel died of cancer.

The death of a loved one is always shattering; the death of a child doubly so because it is, somehow, so radically not in the natural order of things. One can easily imagine, therefore, how many times the experience is tripled and quadrupled when the child one loses is one whom one saw as, in a very real sense, justifying one's own existence. The depth of my father's depression made it clear that he could not survive for long; yet he challenged death (and once more demonstrated his stubbornness) by throwing himself with renewed vigor into *The History of Yiddish*, his own life's work. Practically blind now and very fragile, he nonetheless spent many hours every single day dictating to his faithful secretary and working the text over section by section, polishing footnotes, starting a chapter from scratch, not letting go until it was up to his standards—those same standards that he had faithfully taught to his deceased son. (Eight years earlier, he had written to a friend: "I could, of course, work faster, but to work faster means to lower the quality, and that I will not do. On the contrary, I made a pact with myself that once I sense the quality going down I will stop working.")

My last visit to my father took place in the fall of 1968. It was a year and a half after Uriel's death, and it seemed that in our common grief we had drawn closer to each other. On this particular occasion, the two of us sat together, facing one another on the couch that at night served also as his bed.

"I got a letter from the University of Marburg," he said calmly. "Would you like to see it?" I told him I would indeed.

"Sehr geehrter Herr Professor," it began, in German of course. "In the name of the Rector and Academic Senate, I have the pleasure and honor to invite you, as one of our distinguished alumni, to present six lectures on a theme of your choosing during the next spring term. It goes without saying that, in addition to your hon-

orarium, the University will be pleased to cover all your expenses." It was signed by the Dean of the Faculty of Philology. (I quote to the best of my memory, of course, since I don't have the text before me.)

"Would you like to see my reply?" my father asked. I looked up and saw two huge fires burning in his eyes, and understood. Silently, I reached out and took the carbon copy from his hand.

It was, of course, written in the most flawless, elegant, and masterful academic German I have ever encountered, whose long sentences, stunningly rich in vocabulary and complex in syntax, flowed in a single beautiful and effortless stream; in short, it wrote circles around what the modern Dean, Rector, and Academic Senate put together could have produced. But its content could be readily summarized in one short English sentence: *Go to hell.*

When I looked up again, the fire in my father's almost–blind eyes was gone, and we did not speak of that letter again. He died some months later, on January 29, 1969, having survived Uriel by less than two years; the manuscript of *The History of Yiddish* was finished.

ARRIVAL NOTES

The *President Pierce*, equipped as a troopship and renamed the *Hugh L. Scott*, was sunk by a German submarine on November 12, 1942, off the Atlantic coast of French Morocco. The *Amakusa Maru* was sunk by an American submarine almost exactly two years later, on November 23, 1944, off the east coast of Formosa (now Taiwan); I believe that it, too, was crowded with troops headed for their first combat, probably in the Philippines.

Incidentally, *Amakusa* is the name of an archipelago of small Japanese islands in the general region of Nagasaki, which was an early area of Christianization beginning, probably, with the arrival of Francis Xavier in 1549. Soon thereafter, however, persecutions caused an uprising of Christians in Amakusa, ending in wholesale slaughter. The Episcopal Church commemorates "the Martyrs of Japan" on February 5.

My father's *The History of Yiddish* was published by YIVO in its Yiddish original in 1973. It consists of four volumes totaling well over a thousand pages, of which the first two volumes are text and the remaining two are footnotes. Its terse title contrasts with that of his 1923 Marburg dissertation: translated from the German, it was *Studies on the History and Dialectal Classification of the Yiddish Language Part I: History and Contemporary Status of Yiddish Linguistics.* His final work can, therefore, be considered as Part II of the same project. *The History of Yiddish* has also been published in English translation, but so far minus the footnotes.

PART TWO
The Seeing of My Eye

10 ✀ SCIENCE

People who find out that I am at the same time a physicist and an Episcopal priest invariably want to know how I "reconcile" the two, a question that always makes me smile because I have never in my life, either as an atheist or as a believer, perceived any conflict between the two. The only "disagreements" I have ever seen appeared to be based on some misunderstanding either of science, or of religion, or quite often of both. In view of the frequency with which such questions do arise, however, it seems appropriate to begin this second half of the book, the part to be devoted to questions of faith, with a description of what science has meant, and continues to mean, in my life.

When I was five years old, I once drew a picture of an airplane in cross section. This picture, which I remember quite distinctly, showed the propeller mounted on a shaft that went through two ring bearings and ended in a crank right in front of the pilot's seat. The pilot, in turn, had his hand on the crank. And that's what made the airplane fly through the air.

Grown-ups who saw this picture smiled (just as you are probably doing right now) and assured me that, charming as it may be, that was not actually the method used in real airplanes to keep the propeller in motion. Rather, it was done by a big motor that operated on gasoline. I had heard such rumors before but wasn't interested, because whenever I inquired how the motor worked it turned out, either that people "didn't know the details," or that "it was too complicated for a child like me to understand." As far as I was concerned, only things that I could understand were interesting; being accurate with regard to the "real" world was less important.

My first experience with scientific research came at about that same time. Having recently heard some kind of explanation of electricity, I sat down on the floor in front of an electric outlet (it was the old-fashioned continental style, with two massive prongs an inch or so apart running 220 volts DC), placed two stout nails in the two openings, and put a third nail across them. The result was sublime: whoever would have thought that a very gentle act such as carefully balancing a nail across two others could produce so much sight and sound? Of course people came frantically running from all over the house tearing their hair; later, it was carefully explained to me how easily I could have electrocuted myself, not to speak of setting the house on fire. I listened carefully, understood the message well, but felt no fear or (for that matter) remorse, since I had no intention in any case to repeat the experiment: having found out what happens when one does that, it was time to move on. That's the way scientific research works.

After all, God, too, said "Let there be light" only once.

Although my mother, with her PhD in botany from a German university, was the nominal scientist in the family, I recall my father as taking the larger part in my early scientific explorations; specifically, he would read to us out of various science books for young children. Since this type of literature in Yiddish was limited, he would bring home books in other languages, mostly

German or Russian, and skillfully translate to us at sight. I remember in particular a Russian book entitled *Alyuta the Space
Elephant.* "Space elephant" was used in analogy with, for example,
"sea lion," for a creature that resembles an elephant but resides in
space instead of the African veldt. In the story, the "space elephant," parachuting one day into a playground full of nice boys
and girls (with whom the reader immediately identifies), turns out
to be a pleasant girl dressed in a space suit that resembles an elephant because of the large hose that connects the helmet to a separate oxygen supply. The girl's name is, of course, Alyuta. I don't
recall any of the story, but I know that she immediately makes
friends with a few of the kids on the playground (including me
and Uriel, of course) and goes on to introduce them to the scientific and technical intricacies of space travel. It is Soviet children's
literature at its best.

One way or another, my interest in matters technical—it
would be premature to call them "science"—was firmly established at an early age, and has basically been with me all my life.
Unfortunately, the high school curriculum in New York began
with a full year of what was called General Science, followed by
another year of Biology, neither one of which nurtured my direct
interests in technology. The third year introduced me to chemistry, which I did find quite interesting; but I never got to physics,
because it was offered in the fourth year when I was busy with
other things. The result is that I graduated from high school without really knowing what physics is, and hence without any conscious interest in it.

It's not surprising, therefore, that when I enrolled at the City
College of New York in February of 1945, I chose chemical engineering to be my major: *chemical*, because chemistry was the most
advanced science course I had taken, and *engineering*, because that
ought to be concerned with how things work—which was, after
all, my true interest. But since the chemical engineering curriculum had physics as a required first-year subject, I found myself,
almost accidentally, being introduced to that most compelling
and marvelous discipline; and when I transferred to Columbia
College at the end of that first semester, I took the opportunity to

abandon chemical engineering altogether and opt for physics instead. And so it happened that, in due time, I received my PhD in
physics and spent a full and gratifying life in that profession, finally retiring from my professorship at the University of Michigan
fifty years later.

It is not easy for me to put my finger on what it was about
physics that kept me so consistently fascinated. It begins, I think,
with the way that particular science can, and cannot, be defined.
Whereas one can say that living organisms are the subject of biology, rocks and the earth's structure are the subject of geology,
and the reactions that substances undergo when they come into
contact are the subject of chemistry, physics cannot be specified
by its subject matter. Rather, what defines physics is the very special genre of analogic thinking, leaning heavily on mathematical
expression, that characterizes its method. So, for example, the
word "wave" signifies, in common usage, a certain familiar disturbance of the surface of a body of water; physicists have extended it, first to the transverse disturbance of a stretched string,
then to the pressure disturbances in atmospheric air that constitute sound, and finally to light and other electromagnetic waves,
as well as quantum waves and gravitational waves, which are disturbances in nothing in particular. The point is that there are subtle analogies among the mathematical descriptions of all these
phenomena (although they are by no means the same), the discovery of which sends a physicist into paroxysms of ecstasy. By
definition, then, physics is concerned with those phenomena to
which the method of physics can be successfully applied; or, said
in more abbreviated form, *physics is what physicists can understand*—
a point of view that I already embraced at the age of five in the
way I approached the drawing of an airplane.

Another factor that powerfully attracted me was the nature
of research in general. There are, of course, many human activities whose purpose is to learn to do something that we don't
know how to do; but what characterizes research is that, the moment we have found out how to do a certain task, it becomes no
longer interesting. Research is, in other words, by definition *doing
what one does not know how to do*. As such, it is terribly difficult for

the general public (including, alas, most so-called science writers) to understand, because it appears to those who haven't thought about it as a life of endless frustration. That it does involve lots of frustration is, of course, something that we research scientists know all too well; but we know also that the exhilaration of the occasional moment of success makes it all worth while.

In our present age of computers, the reason for this exhilaration is not all that difficult to understand: after all, whatever you truly know how to do you can program a computer to do for you. In other words, if you can state ahead of time what your response will be to each contingency that may possibly arise within a task (which is the meaning of "knowing how to do" that task), you need merely program those contingencies into your computer and it will perform the task as well as you; better, in fact, because the computer won't make the occasional careless mistakes that you will. But if anything you truly know how to do can be done by a computer, it follows that the only properly human activity is doing what you *don't* truly know how to do. And that (as I found out at the age of five when I put those nails into the electric outlet) is what makes research so exhilarating. It remains the final triumph of the human urge to question whatever is questionable, imagine whatever is imaginable, and comprehend whatever is comprehensible.

When I was a graduate student at Columbia working on my dissertation, there was one professor in the physics department who regularly used to get hot under the collar about what he described as "the dark forces of religion." It is absolutely evil, he proclaimed to all who would listen and some who would not, of the church to impose its ideas on people and tell them what they must believe, thus stifling their capacity for independent scientific thinking. While my general inclination was to agree with him in substance (though not with his manner of expressing it), I was also struck by the fact that there was among my fellow research students in the same laboratory at least one seriously observant Catholic, who in our frequent physics discussions never gave the impression that his scientific talent was in any way impaired. Was the professor's point of view, I began to wonder, not as self-evident as it at first appeared? In fact, was not he himself, who had a justified reputation of outstanding physics discoveries in spite of having a closed mind on the subject of religion, a perfect example of how the one need not affect the other? Right then, I began to suspect that the often-cited "conflict between science and religion" may be based on a lot of misunderstanding, though the nature of that misunderstanding was still far from clear to me.

My own thesis project consisted of a precision measurement of something technically known as "the hyperfine splitting of the metastable triplet state of helium-3." Helium-3 is a rare isotope of helium gas, and Professor Rabi, my thesis advisor, had approved the purchase of three cubic centimeters of the stuff at what then seemed like the astronomical cost of a hundred dollars per cubic centimeter. The work required my collaborators and me to spend long hours in the laboratory seven days a week, nursing a temperamental vacuum system, tending to complex electronics, keeping a high-voltage discharge tube at the correct operating point, and, when all was going well, "taking data" by one of us keeping his eyes glued to a galvanometer in the darkened room while others read off values of various frequencies and magnetic fields and recorded it all in The Laboratory Notebook. After a few months of that, we analyzed our data, found out what was wrong with it, hatched a better idea, rebuilt the apparatus according to this new understanding, and began again. This continued for a number of years, during which our results progressively improved. Finally, I was able to convince Dr. Rabi that they were good enough by pointing out that in order to continue we would need to buy some more of the precious gas, knowing that his frugality would preclude doing that. "OK," he said, "go ahead and write it up." (My final result for the hyperfine splitting of the metastable triplet state of helium-3 was 6735.71±0.05 MHz, a number that means little to most people but still earned me my PhD.)

One evening, as I was tending the apparatus while the others had gone out for supper, I witnessed a very strange phenomenon: all six liquid-nitrogen traps, used to condense unwanted impurities in the vacuum system, simultaneously boiled over. I refilled them, of course (keeping the traps full was in any case one of the jobs of the person monitoring the equipment), but was struck by the fact that I could not, at that moment, think of any explanation for what had happened: a sudden failure of the vacuum could have done it, but the pressure gauges indicated that everything was steady and normal. "I wonder whether that was a miracle," I asked myself with a smile, "the kind that one reads about in the supermarket checkout tabloids?"

But that was just a joke, since I knew that, somewhat paradoxically, in real life observations that appear to violate the laws of physics are a dime a dozen. Every experimental physicist with any experience is aware of that fact. True, there is always the assumption that, if one were to stop and investigate each such "violation," it could perfectly well be explained, but in practice there is usually neither time nor interest for this because the work has to move forward. So, for example, if in a certain situation a milliammeter registers what appears to be a totally absurd value of electric current, the competent physicist may simply replace it with another meter; if the new one behaves more reasonably the problem is considered solved, and the original device is sent to the manufacturer for repairs. Of course, if the replacement meter repeats the same "impossible" value, one must stop and search for an error in the circuit, or in some function of the apparatus, or perhaps in one's understanding of the underlying physics; but if the strange event happened only once it is given no further thought. Even the manufacturer's service department to which the "peculiar" milliammeter is sent may very well decide that the model is too old to warrant the hours that would be required to fix it, so they simply throw it in the trash and substitute a newer model without ever really "explaining" the supposed malfunction of the old one.

This little parable illustrates how, in real life, *science has nothing meaningful to say about a single, unrepeated event.* But this also means that science has nothing meaningful to say, either pro or con, about the parting of the Red Sea, or the virgin birth, or the resurrection of Christ.

It's not that an imaginative scientist is unable, if he puts his mind to it, to think of possible—even if unlikely—hypotheses that could account for such happenings. In the case of my liquid-nitrogen traps, for example, there might have been a patch of loose paint on the ceiling that at the crucial moment—perhaps in response to somebody's heavy footstep—showered a small amount of debris over the apparatus, and the warm particles that fell into the traps would naturally make them boil up. As for the milliammeter, whatever the nature of its supposed misbehavior had been, it is similarly possible to devise a theory (indeed, many theories) that might explain it. The point is rather that retroactively—especially if thousands of years have elapsed—it is seldom possible to find out which, if any, of the proposed hypotheses is correct; and if my Catholic colleague happens to believe that those events were miracles, he cannot be criticized for it on purely scientific grounds *unless, of course, one includes under the heading of "scientific grounds" the belief that miracles do not happen.* It is important to understand, however, that such a belief is not itself established by any kind of scientific proof; rather, it represents the triumphalism of scientists themselves who, intoxicated by their success in explaining in natural terms so many phenomena that had previously been considered supernatural, have recklessly laid claim to everything else in the universe.

For myself, having lived all my life not believing in miracles, I felt no particular compulsion to reconsider at that time; but constant exposure to physics research as a laboratory reality did bring about a subtle change in my thinking. The focus of this change was not, however, in my view of the parting of the Red Sea or any other of what I saw as the charming fairy tales contained in the Old Testament, or of any of the Christian miracles as they are reported in the New, which at the time I had not even read. Rather, my attention was captured more and more by the miraculous nature of physics itself.

To understand what I mean, one needs to understand the difference between an experimental science like physics and an absolute discipline like mathematics. Doing mathematics is like playing solitaire: everything is laid out before you. The imagination of the productive mathematician is expressed in an ability to create new rules, and to make them work consistently with old rules, so as to generate novel and satisfying patterns. But physics is different, in that ultimately whatever rules you try to create must receive the seal of approval that can only be granted by experimental confirmation. Rather than being a game of solitaire, it is a game played against Nature as your opponent: you make a move, then Nature makes a move. Thus the physicist is always trying to outwit an opponent who is infinitely more clever, a task that would be hopeless were it not for one thing: *Nature does not cheat*, but deigns to play the game in a manner accessible to human beings. So, for example, the laws of motion predict that a freely falling projectile fired directly at a freely falling object will hit that object, and a satellite launched according to the same intricately computed laws will land on Mars, and these things actually happen. The physicist's conviction that nature does not cheat, and that if the satellite doesn't get to Mars it is due to a mistake in the physicist's own calculation *that is findable*, amounts to a deep faith in what can only be labeled a miracle. Although the theological language that I am using in thus describing the essence of scientific discovery will amuse many scientists, and perhaps even shock a small number of them, the truth is that few would disagree with the essence of what I am trying to say.

Today, half a century after my graduate student days, I can find no essential fault with those opinions, except that today I would go considerably further. First of all, the entity that I then playfully personified as "Nature" has become much more real to me, having slowly acquired the name "God." Second, I have come to see the relationship embodied in physics research as a basic prototype of how human beings deal with God. It is, after all, true (or so I believe) that God is omnipotent; but if that were the whole story, human life would be nothing but a torrent of wild rapids in which we are caught: we may come out of a particular turn alive, or have our heads smashed on the rocks at God's whim, but our own exertions would, in the face of such power, remain pointless (except, perhaps, as attempts to grovel slavishly for God's favor). If I see the actual situation as very different, it is due to the supreme miracle (some call it "covenant") that *God does not cheat*: there are, indeed, rules, but God, too, abides by them. This self-assumed obligation is not, however, to be seen as an abridgment of divine power: like a loving parent, God may sometimes, under exceptional circumstances, temporarily modify the rules, but always so as to help us learn and grow, not to inject confusion into our attempts to do our part in the covenant.

As to the human urge to question, to imagine, and to comprehend, I now see it as itself part of God's image in which we were created, which prompts us to treat the universe as though we were co-owners of it. The difference between God and us, however, is that we have limitations on what we can comprehend, imagine, and question, whereas God does not. These limitations are, by definition, the boundaries of science: comprehending the humanly comprehensible, imagining the humanly imaginable, and questioning the humanly questionable is what science is about.

Yet still a problem remains with regard to miracles. Granted that science is unable to make a judgment for or against the parting of the Red Sea, the virgin birth, the resurrection of Christ, or any of the other supposedly miraculous happenings that one hears about; yet somehow I—or you—may reach a decision to put credence in some of these but not in others. How we manage to do this will be the subject of later chapters.

11 ∰ BIBLE

Very Thursday morning for a number of years now, Gerane
and I have joined a group of parishioners at Saint Clare's
Church for a session of Bible study, taking as our material
the passages assigned to be read in church during the following Sunday's services. Although the discussion during our ses-
sions is quite freewheeling, there are some things on which the
members of the group, all of us church-going Episcopalians, tend to
agree, perhaps the chief of them being the underlying understanding that the Bible is the Word of God. But such a statement coming
from a person of my background obviously requires explanation.

To begin with: one might expect that growing up in Vilna in
a thoroughly secular setting I would know nothing at all about the
Bible, but that would be naïve. Many stories of the *tanakh* (the
Jewish name for the Old Testament)—the creation, Cain and Abel,

Noah and the flood, the tower of Babel, Joseph and his brothers, the Moses saga, and others—were quite familiar to me; we even read them in school. Far from being regarded, however, as the "Word of God" (which would hardly make sense, since to us secular Jews "God" was not part of reality), they were simply read as fairy tales with, to be sure, some moral content. If they differed in status from "Cinderella" or "The Emperor's New Clothes," it was because of our perception that Bible stories were Jewish, in other words "ours." I think I became aware fairly early that "religious Jews"—those people who were very poor, lived in the slums, and for superstitious reasons maintained anachronistic habits like daily prayer and peculiar dress—actually thought of the Bible stories as true, but that was neither here nor there; gentiles, on the other hand, would surely never even have heard of Abraham or Moses. That there existed Polish kids who, attending their schools just as we attended ours, might have been reading the same stories from an identical (albeit Polish, rather than our Yiddish) Bible that they thought of as theirs, would have struck me as astounding.

But when the war brought our family to New York in the beginning of 1941, I found myself for the first time in my life in an unsegregated society in which all kids went to school together. This does not mean, of course, that I instantly felt close to all my fellow students; indeed, until I started college I cannot recall a single instance of a gentile classmate, male or female, with whom I ever exchanged more than a hello–goodbye. Nonetheless, the idea of wanting to know more about "their" universe suddenly became much more natural, and that's when I found out (probably by putting questions to my father) that the Christian Bible, which "they" regard as a sacred text, consists of two parts called the Old and the New Testament; and that "their" Old Testament is in fact nothing but our *tanakh*. Beyond that, I still had very little information.

In fact, it was not until my early twenties that it occurred to me to take a look at a Bible that included the New Testament as well as the Old, so I ordered one from the Sears, Roebuck mail order catalog, hoping in this way to find out something about the essence of Christianity. The book that arrived (which I still own) was, of course, a King James version, with the words "Holy Bible" embossed in gold on a black leatherette cover that is now quite disintegrated, and a ribbon marker that at one time had the color of bright churchy purple but has now faded to a nondescript gray. Naturally enough, I began by browsing in the English version of the Old Testament, which I generally found quite acceptable. Except for the strange usage of printing each verse as a separate paragraph (which is characteristic of the King James version), the opening chapters of Genesis were exactly as I remembered them from the Yiddish; and I found the English rendition of the twenty-third psalm (which was, as you will see in a later chapter, a favorite of mine) to be decidedly good poetry. But the New Testament was nothing if not puzzling, and generally left me with the uneasy impression that, although it was talking about familiar trees, it all added up to a totally unfamiliar forest. It was, in fact, my first experience of the brick wall that so often separates the people of the two Testaments: Jews, the people of the Old Testament, tend to know absolutely nothing of the New; and Christians, the people of the New Testament, tend radically to misunderstand the Old. Indeed, it was not until a quarter century later that I had occasion to study the Bible sufficiently to make any kind of overall sense out of it.

Because so many people today share this confusion, it seems reasonable to begin with a few objective facts. The Old Testament is a collection of books that were written down (in Hebrew, mostly) over a period of about half a millennium (from about 600 B.C.E. to about 100 B.C.E.). Although there is an immense variation of genres among Old Testament books, their overall theme is the relationship between God and human beings; but more particularly the relationship of God and God's chosen people, which turns out to mean the Jews. No explanation is ever given why God singled out the Jews for this special role; Abraham, from whom all Jews are said to be descended, simply receives a call from God, and the story goes on from there. Throughout, it is made very clear that while being the chosen people is a state of privilege it also carries with it great responsibilities, in that the Jews are expected to act as examples of the image of God in which all of humanity was created, and that their frequent failure to live up to such a standard is, for God, a source of enormous grief. More than once, God becomes angry and exasperated enough to threaten to obliterate the chosen people altogether, but then there is always a change of mind.

The New Testament, whose total length is about one fifth of that of the Old, was written down (in Greek) in about one tenth the time of the Old (roughly from about 40 C.E. until 100 C.E.), and its theme is the life, crucifixion, and resurrection of Jesus Christ and the significance of those events for the salvation of humanity. Its books generally fall into one of only two genres: the Gospels, which narrate the events of Jesus's life, and the Epistles, or letters, which interpret and comment on the essential theological facts of Christianity as their writers understood them. Against the background of the Old Testament, what emerges in the New Testament is a new religion that extends the old one in two essential ways: (a) rather than emphasizing an inviolable divide between the human and the divine, Christianity uses the person of Jesus Christ to explore the continuum that exists between them; (b) rather than emphasizing the relationship between God and "the chosen people," Christianity, again using the person of Jesus Christ, concentrates more on the relationship between God and the individual, and in particular on the individual's need for salvation. This second difference, by the way, turned out to play a critical role in the historical development of Christianity, in that Judaism had always been the unconditional religion of an established group (the Jews), whereas Christianity welcomed converts individually and regardless of background.

Those are the objective facts; but if I set them aside and concentrate on what the Bible has meant to me personally, its most striking characteristic (of which, it is true, I became aware only gradually) has surely been that *the Bible is about me*. When it tells a story, I am each of its characters; when there are long sections in the first person singular (as in the Psalms), I am that person. I am Adam, I am Eve, and I am the serpent; I am Moses, and I am Pharaoh; I am David, and I am Goliath; I am the prodigal son, his father, and his older brother—I know exactly how each of them feels at every moment, whether or not I can recall a similar experience of my own. This ability to identify (which, I know, is shared by other readers) is especially striking since Bible narratives typically spend little time telling us how their characters feel, concentrating mostly on what they do and what they say; and yet I find I have no problem filling in the part that is omitted. But what really astounded me, as I became more and more conscious of my ability to empathize with all of the Bible's characters, was that this ability extended fully to what is in a way the Bible's main character: God.

Right here, I believe, lies one of the Bible's great and powerful paradoxes. Unlike us, God may be omnipotent, omniscient, everlasting, and unwavering in his goodness; as the prophet Isaiah quotes, "My thoughts are not your thoughts, neither are your ways my ways, . . . for as the heavens are higher than the earth, so are my ways higher than your ways, and my thoughts than your thoughts." Yet God never says, "My feelings are not like your feelings," *because,* apparently, *they are.*

It is interesting that the two Testaments deal quite differently with this paradox. The original audience of the Old Testament—the Jews—have lived all of their remembered time with this picture of God, and something which has always been that way ceases to be perceived as a paradox. From the first verses of Genesis, when God says "Let there be light" and *waits to see whether or not the result is good* before proceeding, it is clear that the whole process of creation is for God an exciting adventure of research and exploration being shared with us (even though we are, strictly speaking, not yet there). And when the time does arrive, at the end of the week, to create human beings, "God created humans in his own image, in the image of God he created them"—which, in view of the obvious differences that do exist between people and God, suggests that they are to share *the same feelings,* something that God pronounced as being *very* good. In short, the view of God that emerges throughout the Old Testament is that of a loving parent, infinitely stronger than we and infinitely wiser, and yet composed, somehow, of the same emotional DNA.

But when we consider the gentiles who would become the audience of the New Testament, we can see how difficult they would find it to accept such a view. After all, the gods that existed in the various pagan pantheons, as exemplified by the deities of Mount Olympus, were powerful, emotional, but lacking in morality; whereas the gods that inhabited classical Greek philosophy were powerful, moral, but lacking in emotion. Although at the time of Christ there were, apparently, many gentiles who recognized and admired the special relationship that Jews had with their God (whose nature was clearly governed by all three qualities), they could do no more than be jealous, since the Jewish God—or, as the Jews themselves liked to put it, the only God—had obviously chosen who the special people were to be, and could not be expected to show much interest in anyone else.

The New Testament (written of course by Christians, just as the Old Testament was written by Jews) describes how in response to that, at a certain moment in history, God extended a gracious initiative by sending Jesus Christ into the world, thus creating a channel by which gentiles could feel as lovingly embraced by God as only Jews had felt previously. As the Bible describes it, Jesus was human enough to lack the aloofness of the original Jewish God (who now became God the Father in Christian terminology), and at the same time divine enough to embody God's full authority. The first characteristic—Christ's humanity—is demonstrated by his being born of a human mother, living a full human life of ministry with strong emphasis on helping the poor and otherwise underprivileged, and finally being crucified by the authorities whom he has offended and thus dying an agonizing death. The second characteristic—Christ's divinity—is demonstrated, above all, by the fact that after being fully dead and buried he rises to life again and is, for some time, once more in the company of his disciples before finally ascending to heaven. That is what the New Testament says.

All of which brings us back to the concept "Word of God," which in the beginning of the chapter I claimed to endorse. Does that mean, many readers will impatiently ask, that I take all those statements about God and Christ at face value? Am I, in other words, a fundamentalist who believes in the Bible's literal inerrancy? My answer is "It is, indeed, my sincere belief that everything the Bible tells me is true; but *the hard part is to decide what exactly it is that it tells me."*

This is not a joke, nor a way of evading a difficult question. After all, a text as linguistically and poetically rich as the Bible necessarily contains a lot of metaphor, and few people would demand that "Judah is a lion's whelp," or "My God, my rock in whom I take refuge, my shield, and the horn of my salvation" be taken in their absolutely literal meaning. There are other passages, however, where the answer is not so obvious, for example "Thou shalt not kill": does it mean that we must not slaughter animals for meat? Or shoot a vicious armed intruder in our family's self-defense? Or serve in our country's armed forces in wartime? With regard to each of these questions various opinions are possible, and so interpretation becomes necessary whether we like it or not. What I am saying, in other words, is that in my opinion the fundamentalist view of Scripture as "literally inerrant" is not so much wrong as meaningless; that is, it tells us nothing unless we begin with some preconceived notions of what it is that the Bible teaches. I do not for a moment deny that I too have such preconceived notions; I cannot, however, accept the idea that someone else's are privileged by being "literal" while mine are based on "mere interpretation," since I see those that claim to be literal as being based on interpretation just as much as mine.

My view that the understanding of Scripture depends on interpretation is, incidentally, entirely consistent with Christian (as well as Jewish) tradition, which has never hesitated to imbue the Bible with multiple metaphorical, allegorical, and figurative meanings of great richness and complexity, often relegating the "plain reading" to a definitely subordinate status—to the point that from time to time in the course of history we find theologians pleading not to allow the literal biblical text to be abandoned altogether. This way of looking at the Bible does, however, stand in strong opposition to the way the phrase "literal inerrancy" is interpreted by modern fundamentalists, which is, unlike what many people think, not particularly traditional at all.

Yet until I reached the relatively advanced age of, say, fifty, I simply did not see any of these considerations as in any way "se-

rious." True, the brick wall that I previously mentioned as typically separating people of the two Testaments had already begun,
in my personal case, to melt away, first because I became gradually sensitized to the New Testament's internal logic, and second
because I began to see ways in which the contents of the two
could be made to hang together—though frequently in a manner
that conflicted strongly with that advocated by many traditional
Christian writings. But my expectation that, because of these con-
flicts, "normal" Christians would regard me as a weird heretic did
not materialize; on the contrary, the people with whom, at that
time already, I found myself going to church often considered
what I had to say surprisingly interesting. As a result, I started to
participate more and more in conversations and Bible study
groups that approached the subject in ways that astonished us all.

As part of his or her ordination ceremony, every Episcopal
priest is required to make a solemn public declaration as follows:
"I do believe the Holy Scriptures of the Old and New Testaments
to be the Word of God, and to contain all things necessary to salvation." If truth be told, at the time of my own ordination I still
had very little intellectual understanding of what that statement
might mean—though probably not any less than most other people who go through that ceremony. As the years passed, however,
it all fell more and more into place. Simply put, it means that nobody has a right to tell me what God requires me to do except
God; and insofar as that message comes to me in written form it
comes in the Bible. (Its unwritten form is what we mean by a
sense of morality, and we shall devote the next chapter to it.)

Today, when my friends and I use the phrase "Word of God,"
it has nothing to do with literality or any other legalistic criterion
of how Scripture must be read. It refers, rather, to a perception
that God particularly invites us to pay attention to the Bible because God speaks to us not merely through its actual words but
also through images, thoughts, and ideas that continually come
to us when we contemplate those words and discuss them with
others. Unlike the baseball rulebook or the user's manual for a
washing machine, whose comprehensibility depends only on an
"objective" knowledge of what the words mean, the Bible is an in-

timate document full of revealing allusions and metaphors. In fact, studying the Bible feels a lot like reading a personal letter written to us, whose author's desire for us to understand it is every bit as intense as our own. So we begin to perceive it, not as a detached text written by someone who may as well have retired long ago, but as a conversation among characters whom we know well and with whom we can closely identify, a conversation into which our own thoughts, words, and ideas seamlessly blend.

But precisely for this reason, and again unlike the baseball rulebook or the user's manual for a washing machine, the Bible cannot by itself tell us what to believe. That must remain a matter for faith, a topic we shall not really come to grips with for another four chapters.

12 ❧ MORALITY

Many people see morality and religion as practically synonymous, and feel that one of the important functions—if not the most important function—of going to church is to develop one's sense of morality. Indeed, as a minister I have dealt with a number of young couples who were perfectly comfortable relaxing at home on Sunday mornings (and in many cases freely admitting that "they don't believe any of it") as long as there were no children in the family, yet suddenly feeling the need to be part of a religious community when they became parents "because it is necessary for the children to learn right from wrong." Sometimes, too, the Bible (which is after all regularly read in church) is invoked as being the ultimate rulebook for how human beings ought to behave.

Yet when I was a child growing up in prewar Poland in an entirely nonreligious setting, the idea of morality—in the sense of a strong conception of right and wrong, plus an understanding that "doing the right thing" may on occasion require great personal sacrifice—was clearly embedded in my thinking by the age of four or five. Entering young adulthood, I would say that I had as unambiguous an idea of morality as a person who had been raised in an intensely religious setting; and even today, after nearly twenty years in the Episcopal priesthood, my impression continues to be that the proportion of moral people among those who spend their Sunday mornings at a church service is about the same as in the general population—no more, no less.

Here is an example: In early 1965, just five years after I, a completely secular Jew, came to the University of Michigan, a movement arose for the faculty to strike in opposition to the war in Vietnam. The proposed action had faculty opinion divided down the middle; in addition, the question of whether it is legal for employees of a public university to strike was itself far from clear.

I didn't really know how I felt. On the one hand I was strongly opposed to the war; on the other, the principle that "the faculty *is* the university" was dear to me (especially as I had just been promoted to full professor), and the idea of striking against what is in effect my own family in order to make a political point seemed somehow misguided. I was torn between these two factors and saw no logical way to reason myself out of it until, walking across campus a week or so before the announced strike date, I ran into a close associate who threw down the gauntlet: "Well, Gabi, are you going to strike?"

"Of course," I replied. I was myself taken aback, not to say dumbfounded, by the certainty of my reply, but there it was! I was going to strike.

As a matter of fact, I didn't strike; nobody did. At the last moment, an agreement was reached with university administrators to cancel all classes on the scheduled day and substitute various organized informational activities pertaining to the war (I believe that the English word *teach-in* was coined on that occasion). Still, I will never forget the sudden clarity of feeling with which I realized (a good ten years before I had any conscious interest in religion) that it would be morally right for me to strike, and morally wrong not to. I don't know whether you would have found yourself in agreement with my judgment at that time (half of the faculty did not); I don't even know whether I myself would necessarily reach the same conclusion today. Nonetheless, I am convinced that it is precisely that clarity of feeling that constitutes the essence of morality, and that (on a conscious level, at least) moral decisions need not involve religion at all.

But if it is true, as I believe, that religious and nonreligious people share the same idea of—and investment in—morality, they tend also to share one important misconception, and that is that morality is governed by something called *moral law*. The word "law" does have a number of proper usages in the language, such as *civil law*, which distinguishes "legal" from "illegal," or *mathematical law*, which distinguishes "correct" from "incorrect"; but the phrase *moral law*, purporting to be a set of rules that distinguish "morally right" from "morally wrong," only invites confusion. The reason is that other kinds of law are defined either by citing an exhaustive list of examples or by stating a general principle; in other words, they are fundamentally *deductive*, allowing one to decide a particular case from a general statement of the law. But in my opinion (which would, it is fair to say, be rejected by many theologians) a question of moral right or wrong is fundamentally *inductive* in that it cannot be answered hypothetically; you must be facing a particular, specific, actual case to ask a meaningful moral question, and you then reach your decision on the basis of an inner clarity of feeling rather than by referencing any previously formulated set of rules. This is also known, of course, as "consulting your conscience."

But while the process of making moral decisions certainly does not require thinking in religious terms, I believe that its underlying mechanism does have something to do with God, in that the clarity of feeling to which I have been referring comes from that part of us that is God. That such a part exists I do not doubt, although there are many different ways of describing it. In Old Testament terms, I read it in the statement that human beings, having been created in God's image, acquired the capacity "to know good from evil" by eating of the fruit of the "forbidden" tree. In New Testament terms, the presence of a spark of God in each of us (as well as of a spark of humanity in God) is the fundamental meaning of "incarnation," the belief that Jesus Christ was at the same time totally divine and totally human. Both of those concepts, although not theologically fully synonymous, point to the existence of a kind of "800 number" that gives each human being a direct line to God; and it is through that direct line, in my opinion, that we reach the clarity of feeling by which we can, and do, make moral decisions. That does not mean, however, that faced with a question of morality we simply call that number and are given the answer. On the one hand, the part of us that is God itself reflects God's many-sidedness; on the other hand we are not, after all, God's puppets, any more than our own children are ours (otherwise no disagreement on moral questions could ever arise). Furthermore, the messages that we do receive via the "800 number" can often be clarified by talking them over with friends whom we trust.

For all these reasons, when I am asked, for example, what my position is on abortion (which happens to a minister with fair regularity), I am unable to provide an answer (such as that I am "pro-life" or "pro-choice") that would apply to all hypothetical situations, precisely because the question is one of morality. It can therefore only be definitively answered, in my opinion, by the person concerned listening carefully to the part of her that is God; in this activity, however, I—and other friends—can often be helpful by thoroughly engaging her in conversation. I should again add that, depending on the other person's habits of thought, the word "God" need not explicitly enter our conversation at all.

It should be clear from these examples that I personally have no trouble dealing with people whose moral choices are in some respects different from mine; I don't feel that I need to accept those other choices or to refrain from arguing against them. I do, however, expect others to share one particular moral conviction of mine, and that is the need for people to respect each other in spite of their moral disagreements. Such disagreements arise naturally, after all, because of God's many-sidedness and because of human creative independence.

There are, however, truly difficult cases in which my 800 number fails me, as in this example.

On May 23, 1944, my brother Uriel turned eighteen and was drafted into the army; he then was given one furlough at the end of his basic training and another in the late spring of 1945 after graduating from Officer Candidate School and receiving his commission. At that point he was of course in superb physical shape, lean and taut like a well-tuned piano string, and I was awed (as any kid brother would be) by the number of push-ups he could do every morning. I also knew, as did we all, that his next assignment would be overseas.

By then I was seventeen, and Uriel took me into a tavern and ordered two beers, whose bitter taste I had never until then particularly tolerated. "One should learn to drink beer," he said, and suddenly it tasted wonderful. When we returned home we were joined in the elevator by another young man, in the uniform of a private, who saluted smartly. "Where are you stationed, soldier?" Uriel calmly inquired, and the young man replied, "Fort Dix, sir." Uriel nodded, and my pride was indescribable. "We are an officer" ran through my mind while I worked hard to keep a straight face. "Not only do we have a gold bar on our collar, we also know how to behave toward subordinates with authority and self-confidence."

By the time Uriel's overseas assignment came through, the war in Europe was over; nonetheless he was not sent to the Pacific, where fierce fighting continued, but to Germany to join the army of occupation—perhaps because of his facility with European languages.

Always a faithful correspondent, Uriel kept the family supplied with one or two long letters a week starting with the day of his induction. When company was present—especially on Tuesday evenings, which for years functioned in our household as literary gatherings at which we all took turns reading passages from Yiddish literature, both old and contemporary, that my father selected—my father also read excerpts from Uriel's most recent letters. He was, after all, the first live representative of our circle to descend into the hell that had been Nazi Germany, and his reportage was eagerly devoured.

I remember particularly his description of an incident that happened in Kassel, where for a while he had the job of locating and requisitioning officers' living quarters. Having found a particularly attractive private residence he informed the owner that he was being evicted, but the man continued to give him a hard time even after the situation had been thoroughly explained (Uriel's command of German was, of course, excellent).

"So I grabbed him by the collar and threw him down the stairs," wrote Uriel to his loving family.

That moment is chiseled in my memory as are few others. There were seven or eight of us listening to that letter trying our best to look solemn, yet we were all suppressing an urge to scream "Hurray" and embrace each other because we knew, *knew for a fact*, that this *disgusting pig of a Nazi* was lucky to have gotten away with a mere *express trip down his own disgusting staircase*, and if by chance his neck happened to get broken in the process *so much the better!* My grandmother was lined up at the edge of one of the large pits in Ponar (in the forest outside Vilna) along with tens of thousands of other Jews from the just liquidated ghetto and calmly machine-gunned from behind so that the bodies would topple into the pit (the details were known from the witness of a few victims who, not quite dead, crawled out from the tangle of bodies when night fell and miraculously survived). Every one of us listening to Uriel's letter had a collection of such personal stories, stories not only of death (which sometimes seemed the least of it) but of endless abasement and dehumanization at the hands of Germans who were, in turn, endlessly amused by how easy it was to dispose of Jews. But now, at last, revenge came at the hands of this nineteen-year-old second lieutenant in crisp American khaki acting for us and for millions of others; he was self-confident, beautiful, courageous, strong, and instinctively knew the right tone to take with a German. He was our hero and our champion.

He was, of course, also my brother, and in all the years that I knew him (he died at the age of forty) I never encountered a kinder or gentler boy or man. Although he acknowledged no re-

ligious faith, today it is obvious to me that the spark of divinity
that we all have within us by virtue of having been created in
God's image, and which is at the center of our sense of morality,
was active in Uriel as in few other people. Yet his behavior in
Kassel nearly sixty years ago, which at the time had my whole-
hearted admiration, would strike me today (if it happened today)
as crude, cruel, and, yes, immoral. "Vengeance is mine; *I* will repay,
says the Lord": it seems to me today that if that German house-
holder did, indeed, deserve that kind of punishment, God could
damn well be the one to mete it out, and I would have none of it.

It is one of the major regrets of my life that, in the two
decades that passed between that incident and Uriel's death, I
never once asked him about it. For myself, I know the abhorrence
that I feel at any narrative of the Holocaust, and especially at
movies or TV programs made by people who were not there
themselves but recognize its great entertainment value. It does
not entertain me. The only writings that I can stomach—that I in
fact long for—are original sources describing Jewish humiliation
and suffering. Lacking the strength to endure much of it at a time,
I still regularly experience a powerful need to read them.

Unfortunately, there are only a small number of people in my
life with whom I can talk about any of this, and Uriel, had he not
died, would have been one of them. How did he feel throwing
that man down the stairs? Did he think about it later? Did the
concepts of morality become any clearer in his mind after that, as
I wish they had done in mine?

And what questions would he then have put to me in return?

13 ✤ MUSIC

In parallel with my interest and devotion to technical things, music has also always occupied a place of honor in my heart, as an apparent right–brain counterpoise to my general left–brain predisposition. And even though music has often needed to fight an uphill battle in this engagement, I don't believe I could have come to faith without it.

To go back to the beginning: Since time immemorial there stood in our living room in Vilna a very handsome black upright piano, which I early discovered was capable of making character-istic and interesting noises if one raised the lid and depressed the keys (which came in black and in white). When I reached the age of inquiring how and why various objects got there, I was told that at one time long ago my mother actually played that piano; naturally, I then insisted that she show me. At first she refused, pleading that she had forgotten how, but when I continued to exert pressure she finally sat down and played a very poor scale. Then and there I made a mental note not to test her that way again: if she claims to be unable to do something, she is most likely telling the truth.

When I was five years old, it was announced that Uriel (who was seven) would start getting piano lessons. Soon afterwards a young woman named Miss Nadel began to visit once a week, sit with Uriel at the piano, and show him not only how to make interesting sounds but even to play little pieces. I was up in arms: Why can he get piano lessons and not I? "Because," my mother replied, "you wouldn't practice." "How do you know? I will *so* practice!" This went on week after week, until at length she relented; so Miss Nadel began to come twice a week, and I started my first piano lessons. I was very excited about this and greedily drank up everything she told me—until she got to how important it was to practice scales every day, which I took to be a great exaggeration. As a result, my lessons were discontinued after a few months because I didn't practice.

In fact I had, at that early age, already developed the trait of believing (incorrectly) that there was *nothing* that I needed to practice because I could always employ my brain in place of physical skill. The results were not, of course, always satisfying: I would have dearly loved to play ball at recess like the other boys, but because I lacked that skill, I was always chosen last for any team. Some years later in New York, after my first summer at camp, during which I found out yet again that I was incapable of throwing or catching a ball, I resolved to come back the following year as a star pitcher. To carry out this plan, the first thing I did upon returning to the city in the fall was to obtain my own softball; after which, every evening right after supper, I would go down to a neighborhood empty lot, draw a strike zone on a wall with chalk, and begin to practice. Unfortunately, it soon became clear that I had a long way to go and that the days were rapidly getting shorter, so I gave up the endeavor.

The problem with my early piano lessons was similar: I insisted on treating music (in good Platonic fashion) as a purely intellectual discipline. To some degree the fault lay with my parents, in that I was never, for example, taken to a concert, or otherwise exposed to the sound of serious music. (High-fidelity phonograph recordings were still a matter of the distant future, and I cannot recall the radio, itself something of a novelty, being used for anything except listening to the news.) That's why I will never forget the day when Boba (our grandmother) stopped by for a visit and casually sat down at the piano, opened the lid, and proceeded to give a fluent, and as far as I could tell flawless, performance of Chopin's C-sharp minor waltz. I was utterly dumbfounded. Of course I had no idea Boba had that talent (in fact, she belonged to a generation whose well-to-do young ladies were thoroughly trained in "young ladies' accomplishments" such as this); but, much more important, it was the first time that I heard *real music* rather than the tinkly five-finger exercises that comprised Uriel's lessons. "Come and listen to Boba play!" I called to my mother. "She sounds like an orchestra!"

Since learning to play Uriel's rather primitive pieces apparently required an hour's practice every day, making it clear that learning to play like Boba would mean practicing even more than that for many years, I needed to find an alternative path to music, so I decided to be a composer. My first composition was a funeral march of eight measures, which, at my mothers's suggestion, I showed to Mr. Teytlboym, the music teacher at school. Mr. Teytlboym was a young man who came into our classroom once a week and taught us songs, accompanying himself, and us, on his concertina; he also combed his hair in a manner I greatly admired and tried to emulate. When I handed him my eight-measure manuscript he hummed it to himself—again impressing me greatly, since I hadn't known that it was possible to "read" music without spreading it out on the piano and picking out the notes one by one—and then complimented me on my composition, making his position as my idol even more secure.

I don't remember how far I got with my musical self-education in grade school, except that music did become an important part of me, and has remained so ever since. I do know that when the war started and the Russians requisitioned our apartment we also lost the piano, because Boba's apartment, into which we then moved, was far too crowded with refugees from Warsaw to allow space for it. But a year or so after the nuclear family was reunited in New York, Uriel and I decided that, together, we would buy a piano and locate it in our bedroom. I don't recall whether our parents subsidized the purchase, but I do know that the two of us energetically saved our allowances until we were able to buy a used upright piano for twenty-five dollars.

This piano was a source of great satisfaction and joy for both Uriel and me, but as time went on Uriel's other interests drew him progressively away, whereas my devotion to music became ever stronger, and I taught myself to play more and more serious pieces. Two summers later, at the age of fifteen, I went as a junior counselor to a summer camp where I met a shabbily dressed but nonetheless distinguished-looking elderly gentleman by the name of Mr. Jacobson, who was employed to play march music on a frightfully decrepit and out-of-tune old piano as the kids filed into the dining room. When I got to chat with him it turned out that, years earlier (he was older than my father), he had been a student at the Saint Petersburg Conservatory and studied composition with the great Nikolai Rimski-Korsakov before moving on to Berlin and receiving further lessons from Engelbert Humperdinck; now, however, he had obviously fallen on hard times. Back in the city in the fall, I arranged to take weekly instruction from him at three dollars per lesson (which came out of my own pocket), but stubbornly made it clear that I really wasn't interested in piano lessons that would require me to practice; rather, I wanted to study harmony, counterpoint, and composition. When some time later I showed one of my completed fugue exercises to Mr. Ross, the music teacher and organist at George Washington High School, he liked it so much that he volunteered to perform it as part of an assembly program presented by the school's mathematics club (of which I was, of course, a member), with the somewhat flimsy excuse that fugue is a rather mathematical type of music. He also requested, and obtained, my permission to play it at his church the following Sunday, where (he later told me) it was very well received.

Although both my parents were naturally proud of my creative accomplishments, they also each had strong reservations. In my mother's case, her innate self-discipline told her that to learn music without the usual hours and hours of tedious practice had to have something sinful about it. By contrast my father, himself quite tone deaf and with no ear for music at all (although he did love poetry, and had in his youth translated large sections of the *Iliad* from the original Greek into Yiddish while maintaining the original hexameter), was more worried about my teacher's unverified credentials—especially as Mr. Jacobson appeared to be supportive of my unorthodox agenda of learning advanced topics in music theory without studying an instrument. (In fact, Mr. Jacobson told me more than once that it would be good for me at least to be able to play my own exercises, but he was not prepared to lose a talented student over this issue.) At length I graduated from high school and no longer had time for private lessons, whereupon my father urged me to take stock of what I had learned by consulting Dr. William Miller, one of the theory professors in the Columbia music department, with whom he had recently established contact for this purpose. Dutifully, but with a beating heart, I did so, taking along a portfolio of my recent work including a transcription of Beethoven's Appasionata Sonata as a piano concerto with full orchestra accompaniment (along with my rationale for why this particular sonata is better scored that way than for Beethoven's original solo piano), plus some recent exercises in seven-part strict counterpoint with each part notated in a different clef. Professor Miller was duly impressed, and said that he would like to have me join his graduate music theory seminar except that it demanded, as a prerequisite, at least one year of undergraduate theory. So I took Professor Miller's intermediate harmony class as a college freshman, and his graduate theory seminar as a sophomore—all this while following the normal course sequence of a student majoring in physics.

Yet the fundamental issue dogged me. Deep down, I knew that what I wanted to do was not just to *understand* music but to *make* music; that is, to engage not only my intellect but the rest of my body, which does require actual physical practice. Of course I must actually have been practicing quite a bit, or I could not have mastered various pieces by Bach, Beethoven, and Chopin to the extent that I had; but I wanted to *excel* at it, to be the person who, at the dimming of the lights in Carnegie Hall, comes on stage to thunderous applause and then, as silence falls, gives a performance of Bach, Beethoven, or Chopin that is so truly breathtaking that the audience remembers it for years to come.

One is tempted to dismiss such thinking as adolescent fantasy —which, of course, it was; but it does also involve a deep paradox, one that I did not fully verbalize until fifteen or twenty years later. By then I was settled in Ann Arbor, owned a beautiful seven-foot Steinway grand, and regularly played chamber music with friends; and I was impressed by how immensely enjoyable it was to do that—in spite of the fact that our performances, when compared with recordings of professionals obtainable at any music store, were at best terribly mediocre. Time after time, with the pretext of learning something from our mistakes but in fact with the hope of re-experiencing our wonderful playing, I would set up my tape deck and record every minute of the evening—only to find out on playback the next day that the "wonderful playing" was, like the ghost in an attempted photograph, not actually there.

As I consider this from the perspective I have today, I can see a theological explanation for it. We all have in mind, for each possible activity, an ideal of perfection—which is essentially what we mean by *God.* We also have within us, for each possible activity, an urge to imitate this ideal—which is what we mean by *being in the image of God.* We cannot help the fact that we are not God, and therefore do not live up to our ideal of perfection; nor can we help having been created in the image of God, which makes us constantly *try to* live up to that ideal. My problem when I was young was, quite simply, that I was confusing the two.

In the field of music performance, there do exist a relatively small number of people who, to the rest of us, themselves embody perfection: for them, no such thing as technical difficulty seems to exist. These are the virtuosi who come on stage to thunderous applause and give that breathtaking performance of Bach, Beethoven, or Chopin that the audience remembers for years to come. Of course it isn't really true that everything is easy for them, but because they are so far advanced beyond the rest of us they can function as reminders, or *icons*, of perfection.

When we hear a performance by an artist of that caliber, the joy we experience is the *joy of perfection*, a reminder of God. But when, for better or for worse, we ourselves play the same piece, what we experience is *the joy of being in the image of God* and doing our best to *imitate* perfection—rather than entertaining any idea of ourselves being perfect. This is the fundamental reason why the first can be recorded and still, upon being played back, remind us of God; whereas the second, when recorded and played back, reminds us of nothing except the imperfect happenings of the previous evening.

Somewhere near the middle of my academic career, I was asked by the physics department at Michigan to teach a course in the Physics of Music directed at a wide audience including science or engineering majors, music majors, and others in unrelated specializations who simply had an interest in the subject. It was actually a question by a student in that class—"Why is it that most piano hammers are designed to hit more than one string?"—that led me to the realization that the field of musical acoustics could provide a fruitful area for original physics research. My first investigation, into the coupling of multiple piano strings, did not just produce the answer to my student's question but simultaneously signified an important change in my professional life: not only were the results of that research published in the *Journal of the Acoustical Society of America* and then again as a cover story in *Scientific American*, but the work also led to generous funding by the National Science Foundation. Subsequently I widened my interest to the physics of other musical instruments, notably to instruments of the violin family, where my work became widely known and earned a number of awards.

∞

Since the spring of 1991, I have known that my brain contained a slowly growing tumor, which was, at the time of its discovery, the size of a pingpong ball; in subsequent years it grew slowly but steadily to the size of a tangerine, and as I write this (August 2002), I am three months into recovery from the operation that finally removed it. In the days immediately following the surgery the whole right side of my body was completely paralyzed; about a week later, I remember watching in awe as I was actually able to move my right thumb about an eighth of an inch. Today, my longhand writing is still clumsy and tense, and when I sign my name it is a far cry from what I have known for well over half a century to be my signature.

When I came home from the three-week sojourn in the hospital leaning on my walker, the first request I made was that the piano be opened; I then sat down and tried to play a C major scale, but no scale emerged. True, it looked as though most fingers came down on or near the correct keys, but not only was the timing totally uncontrolled but the forces were so irregular that some notes sounded *fortissimo* but most did not sound at all. I cried, just as I had done in the intensive care unit when, on the day after surgery, I found that my paralysis had not improved. But looking at the piano now, I suddenly remembered Miss Nadel's injunction to practice, and so I practiced; after ten minutes I was exhausted, but a very vague outline of what I wanted to hear could by then be heard.

The following day I again sat down at the piano and, after some minutes of practicing the same scale, reached (with considerable difficulty—I didn't want to topple over since I was not holding on to my walker) for the Bach Two–Part Inventions. After all, I reasoned, what I am practicing is not the scale itself but the simple ability to control the force and the timing of a finger to produce a sound, so the sound may as well be interesting! Fifteen minutes later I had laboriously gone through the first Invention and burst out crying again, but this time in joy and relief. "Did you hear that?" I cried to Gerane. "I actually made some music!"

Now three months have passed since my surgery, and I have begun to work on my book again. (The computer keyboard is, of course, vastly more forgiving than that of the piano: if one makes a mistake at the computer, one can always delete or correct it without leaving a trace, a feat that is not possible when playing music!) Indeed, I am already immensely thankful that the creative function of my brain does not seem to have been appreciably impaired; in fact, my encounter with eternity on the operating table may have actually expanded it. Hopefully, some of my new insights will appear in the few chapters that remain.

As far as the piano is concerned, the final outcome is still unknown. When I was writing earlier in the chapter about Boba visiting us in Vilna and fluently playing Chopin's C-sharp minor waltz, I went over to the piano and tried playing it myself; what came out could not even be called a parody. Even though my mind clearly knew what was *supposed* to happen, my fingers simply *could not remember* how to do it. But then it had, after all, taken Boba many years of practicing scales—yes, scales—to get to her stage of playing. Of course she had the advantage of never having had brain surgery; but I have the advantage of all the intellectual understanding of music that I accumulated in all those years of *refusing* to practice, while composing seven-part strict counterpoint and fugues that I myself could not possibly play.

Perhaps the time has now come to catch up, both on practicing and on remembering. And remembering, with a vengeance, is what the next chapter is about.

14 ❧ CRUCIFIXION

C rucifixion was a Roman way of killing people they didn't like, by nailing their hands and feet to a large wooden cross and allowing them to hang until they died, typically a matter of many hours. It combined physical torture, capital punishment, and the odium of public humiliation in a single horrendous act.

Today, our minds tend to boggle at such unbridled sadism; yet when the people who drew up our Bill of Rights barely over two centuries ago decided to include in it a prohibition against "cruel and unusual punishment," this was, even then, by no means an idle injunction. Indeed, those who consider it self-evident that potential criminals can always be deterred by the threat of punishment have no choice, when their theory appears to be violated, but to clamor for more severe sentences, not stopping at the more or less arbitrary limit of death but continuing to search for ways of making the culprit wish for death as a welcome alternative. It is not suprising, therefore, that two thousand years ago such an approach was seen as perfectly normal.

On a certain spring Friday in the thirties of the first century C.E., Jesus of Nazareth, an itinerant Jewish preacher from Galilee, was crucified in Jerusalem. Two others—criminals, apparently—were crucified along with him, but they have remained tiny bit players in the world's consciousness. By contrast, the crucifixion of Jesus Christ (as Jesus of Nazareth is more generally known) is regarded as an important occurrence in world history and, by Christians, as a central cosmic event in God's working out of his plans for the salvation of humanity. The reason why Christians are able to perceive it that way does not, of course, begin with theological theory (which came later), but with the human emotions that the event is capable of engendering.

The first of these emotions is *identification:* it is possible for all of us to experience Christ's agony on the cross as our agony since, to use the Gospel phrase, we all have our crosses to bear. For the Christian this is, I believe, a constructive and helpful emotion. Pain is easier when it is perceived as being shared, and much easier when it is perceived as being shared by God (which, in the Christian view, is what Jesus Christ is). After all God, who is omnipotent, would not suffer without *choosing* to suffer; and if God chose to suffer it must be because that suffering has a purpose, and therefore so does mine.

I once knew an experienced obstetrician whose way of reconciling what she witnessed as the obviously considerable pain of childbirth with the fact that many mothers happily engaged in repeat performances was that pain is something we are incapable of remembering: no matter how severe it is at the time, that severity is soon forgotten. (She had no children herself.) I can't agree with that view, however, because of the many counter-examples that I know, cases in which the memory of some past great anguish is so vivid as to turn it into an absolute obsession. No, the reason why so many mothers decide to have more than one child is less a matter of *denying the pain* than of *affirming the purpose.* Whatever its severity—and it does, apparently, vary with the individual woman—the distress of childbirth pales compared to the exaltation that comes from the result.

All of which leads me to some reminiscences.

Alisa, my first wife, and I had been married eighteen years, and had two delightful small children aged eight and six, when in the spring of 1969 she decided to leave us. The fact is, however, that her whole life had been, in one way or another, tormented. She had been born into a wealthy Viennese Jewish family, a family that had flourished in the rich culture known to us through names such as Sigmund Freud, Artur Schnitzler, Egon Schiele, Oskar Kokoschka, and Arnold Schönberg. In fact, however, those were all exceptions, fiercely rebellious creative souls who, in unfaltering individuality, swam resolutely against the stream of conservative and authoritarian Viennese bourgeois society that rejected them all. At the time of the German *Anschluss* of Austria in 1938, Alisa's family emigrated and ultimately settled in Los Angeles; she and I met in 1948 and married in 1951. Shortly after that, Alisa's father divorced her mother who, not being able to find her way alone, jumped out of a hotel window a few years later. Within another year or two, Alisa's younger brother (and only sibling) shot himself. Alisa's father never visited the cemetery where either one was buried; he told me he didn't like cemeteries.

When I met Alisa, she belonged to a Zionist youth movement whose members planned to emigrate and settle in Palestine, or Israel as the brand-new state was now called. I'm not sure to what degree her decisions were due to my influence, but after meeting me she opted to abandon her expatriation plans and resume her college education instead. She did earn an undergraduate degree at the New School for Social Research in New York, and started graduate work in sociology at Columbia, but was never able to do a dissertation and abandoned that project also.

In 1960, we moved to Ann Arbor, where our beautiful son Dan was born. Two years later, his equally beautiful sister Becky came along. For a while it seemed that Alisa could be happy in her motherhood, but apparently the joy of taking care of infants did not fully extend into the time when the children were becoming real people. After that she attempted first writing, then making and selling ladies' clothing of her own design. Nothing worked. Decades of psychotherapy with a long string of therapists had kept her intellectually engaged but seemed unable to touch a deeper emotional level.

Finally, she decided that she wasn't really meant to be living in a family situation, and abandoned that "project" also. With a wonderful father like me, she told me, the children too would be better off without her for a mother. So in the spring of 1969 she rented a tiny downtown apartment and moved out. Her idea was that the small inheritance she had from her mother would be enough for her to live on until she got herself established as a writer and/or fashion designer. But a year later the money was gone, and neither career was showing any signs of taking off, so she ingested a bottle of prescription sleeping pills that she had apparently been hoarding for this purpose. She didn't die, but spent close to a week in a coma. The hospital, knowing the over-whelming probability of a failed suicide repeating the attempt, would not discharge her without someone releasing it from legal responsibility. This was done by two sets of very devoted friends, with each of whom she could stay for some time. Indeed she did that, for a total of four weeks I believe, then was allowed to re-turn to her apartment. She telephoned me then, and said that she wanted to talk. She felt that she had lost her way, and would like to return home and try again.

My ensuing visit to her was surely the most heartbreaking encounter of my life. I knew her well enough to recognize that, although she spoke in good faith, she had not in fact gone through any radical internal transformation. She still had in her a streak of real violence that would, I felt, make it unsafe to have the children in her care. I also had enough experience to know, as well as the hospital, the virtual certainty of her following up with another, probably more successful, suicide attempt. And fi-nally, after eighteen years of being a strong man caring for a weak woman who lacked the capacity to reciprocate my love, I felt that it was time to start getting my own life in order.

So I declined her request, explaining that for me to take her back would be like remarrying, and at that moment I simply wasn't ready to marry anybody. "But look at it this way," I said, "for many years you have labored under the jinx of suicide, feeling destined to follow in your mother's and brother's path. But now the curse is broken! You did commit suicide, but you survived! For the first time in your life you are free to start afresh." Suddenly, her face had more color than I had seen for a long time; her eyes shone, and a real smile played on her lips. "Do think about it," I said, and took my leave. A few days later she sat down at her desk, cut the arteries of her wrists and throat, and died. Alisa's father did not come to the funeral because he didn't like cemeteries.

During that period, neither Alisa nor I had any faith in the conventional sense of the word. But there was a great difference between us in that Alisa had never, in her whole life, been able to discern *any* purpose in her suffering. (Whether that suffering was "real" or "imagined" is, of course, meaningless to ask: pain that is felt is, by definition, real.) That's why her life was continually punctuated by projects that she pursued with an almost messianic zeal—Palestine, marriage, sociology, psychoanalysis, children, writing, fashion design—always looking for the one magic solution that would bring meaning to her existence and, therefore, purpose to her suffering. When she ran out of projects, there was nothing for it but to call it quits.

My situation was different. My professional research had ground to a halt and, after she moved out, I spent most evenings, once the children were asleep, sitting alone and drinking hard, regularly going through two or three bottles of bourbon a week. But in spite of occasional moments of profound despair, I also knew there was a real purpose in my life, and that purpose was the children. It was, so to speak, my own experience of childbirth, the distress of which pales compared to the exaltation that comes from the result. And so, unlike her case, there never was any question that I would make it through, and I did.

Of course most of us, especially by the time we reach a certain age, have found out what it means to make great sacrifices for those we love, and know the enormous strength with which such a purpose can endow us. Yet the same idea means very little when we need to face the myriad kinds of suffering that are part of our lives but do not lead, in any obvious way, to results that are at all joyful or exhilarating. The ravages of war or famine, the loss of a child, a family torn apart by hatred, the curse of a chronically excruciating disease—left to ourselves, it's hard, if not impossible, to see any good in any of them. But if I can perceive my own agony as being part of Christ's agony on the cross, which must have had not just a purpose but one of cosmic proportion, then that purpose must flow over to my suffering also; it may not decrease the intensity of the pain, but it does radically change its flavor, making it much more bearable. Moreover, for this to happen does not require my having a full understanding of what God's purpose in the crucifixion was, only a conviction that such a purpose exists. And that is the first important emotion that comes to the Christian upon contemplating the cross, and one which, as I said, I see as entirely positive and constructive.

But then there is the other, more problematic, emotion that is, in the Christian at least, also awakened by the same contemplation, and that is the emotion of guilt. Indeed, one of the first things that struck me when, a few years after Alisa died, I began to accompany Gerane to church as an interested outsider was the frequency with which guilt, and general self-deprecation, was mentioned in the liturgy. Every Episcopal service includes a General Confession, in which the people kneel and, in a clear loud voice, say terrible things about themselves: *"We have followed too much the devices and desires of our own hearts. We have offended against thy holy laws. We have left undone those things which we ought to have done; And we have done those things which we ought not to have done; And there is no health in us."* (This is from Morning Prayer, but the Communion service is not any less severe; likewise, this is from the Book of Common Prayer that was then in use, but the current one pretty well repeats it.) When I asked the rector why Christians seemed to have so much self-hate in them, he really had no good answer except to say that he, too, deplored it, and that he wished something would be done to remove it.

Yet in terms of classical Christian theology, the connection between feelings of guilt and the crucifixion is very old. Saint Paul, writing in the First Letter to the Corinthians not much more than twenty years after the event itself, says: "For I handed on to you as of first importance what I in turn had received: that *Christ died for our sins* in accordance with the scriptures. . . ." This appears to say that, had we not sinned, there would have been no need for Christ to die, meaning that *the crucifixion is our fault*. Under the circumstances, who could possibly *not* feel guilty? And yet classical Christian theology is here pointing at what is in fact a much more widespread emotional connection.

Consider my own case: I was not in any regular contact with Alisa after her first suicide attempt, apart from that one time when I had gone to see her at her initiative. I did, however, a few days later get a call from mutual friends when she was, apparently, expected for dinner there, failed to show up, and was not answering her phone. Getting no information from me, they went to her apartment and found her. By then, my heart was telling me clearly what the next telephone call would be, and when it came, *I instantly felt like a murderer*. If only I had done *this!* If only I had done *that!* Instead, I have followed too much the devices and desires of my own heart! I have offended against God's holy laws! I have left undone those things which I ought to have done, and have done those things which I ought not to have done!

Of course I was not at that time a Christian, and the contents of the Book of Common Prayer were still completely unfamiliar to me, so that it is not likely that I would have verbalized my feelings in those precise words. Yet most of us know the degree to which any death of a person to whom we were close awakens in us a sense of guilt ("I had been meaning to write her a comforting letter but never got around to it. Now it's too late"), and how much more intense that sense becomes when the death is a suicide. On such occasions, I have often heard people comment on what a good emotional "fit" they find in the words of the General Confession which, like piano music written by a composer who was himself a pianist, naturally "falls under the fingers." This illustrates what some modern Prayerbook reformers do not always understand, and that is that the power of liturgy can finally only be effective if it begins by *meeting us at the point where we are*. In my experience, the General Confession does not make us feel guilty;

rather, by acknowledging the guilt that we so often experience from other causes, it can, when it functions well, give us a hand in getting up off our knees and receiving God's love instead.

The way this works is, however, a bit complicated. What happens first, after the Confession has been recited, is that the priest stands before the congregation and pronounces absolution. He or she does not *give* absolution, which would imply that there is, for the priest, some choice in the matter; there is not. In effect, the people are simply *reminded that God has already forgiven them.*

But in fact that is not exactly correct either. For in spite of the popular saying that "To err is human; to forgive, divine," I personally believe that forgiveness, too, is a human invention: God does not forgive because, from God's point of view, there is nothing to forgive. Just imagine a parent's reaction (yours, if you are a parent) to your child doing something wrong: typically, it might make you sad, or troubled, or angry, but forgiveness would, except in very rare cases, be beside the point because it would mean *reinstating your child in your love,* which was never withdrawn. Now try to extrapolate from yourself to God, whose love is infinite, and you will understand that God's love *can never be withdrawn,* and therefore God can never "forgive." In my opinion (and I must admit that here I deviate considerably from most standard theology) God sometimes offering forgiveness to us is what I, as a priest, would call a *pastoral* gesture, something to allay our intense anxieties until a more permanent solution to the problem can be found.

Which brings us back to First Corinthians, and Paul's statement that "Christ died for our sins." Although it is all too easy to read it as "the crucifixion was my fault," that is not what it says to me. Rather (and in this case many mainline theologians would agree) Paul's phrase "our sins" refers not to this or that individual transgression but to *original sin,* a quality that we all share and that is not, in any simple way, under our control. It is the compulsion to try to interpret anything bad that happens as somebody's fault and, failing that, to conclude that it must be our own. As a corollary, it is the inability to perceive suffering as anything other than punishment—if not the sufferer's, then ours. But in reality "Christ died for our sins" means that *Christ died to free human-ity from original sin;* in other words the crucifixion, far from being anyone's fault, was one of God's great and self-sacrificing attempts to repair that particular catastrophe of creation.

Yet whereas Paul, and other early Christians, spoke joyfully of the incarnation, crucifixion, and resurrection of Jesus Christ as resulting in the greatest transformation the universe has experienced since its creation, there is little clear evidence of such a transformation in the world around us today. War, pestilence, hatred, and violence among nations, as well as greed, disease, prejudice, and cruelty among individuals—they all seem to be about as prevalent today as history tells us they were before Christ's appearance. And it would certainly seem that *original sin*, the cancer of the conscience that has been part of the human condition since creation, continues to be rampant.

Still, God has not given up; but to understand the meaning of that statement we will finally need, in the remaining three chapters, to confront the question of faith head-on.

15 ❧ FAITH

In a technological age such as ours, there is a tendency to consider scientific knowledge to be the only real knowledge, even (or perhaps especially) by people who do not properly understand what "scientific" means. Faith is then seen as being opposed, if not indeed subordinated, to science: science comprises what we "really know," whereas faith is what we "merely believe." Considering that science has been with us for only four centuries or so while the origin of faith is lost in prehistory, there is obviously some danger in limiting ourselves to a mode of thinking that relegates faith to the status of a kind of second-rate science. As a more useful description, I would suggest that science is *knowledge of the part of the universe that we understand*, whereas faith is *an acknowledgment of the part of the universe that we don't understand*. Defined in this way, it is clear that faith enlarges our view of the world rather than diminishing it.

The division of the universe into a part that we understand and a part that we don't is, of course, not the same for all human beings. Little children, for example, receive almost everything on faith, because we as their caretakers try to protect them from objective evidence of what will happen if (for example) they climb way up on the side of their crib. As a result we simply teach them not to do it, either giving no reason at all or else a "reason" that they are not in a position to understand or evaluate. Adults, on the other hand, can clearly see objective arguments for not crossing a busy thoroughfare with eyes closed; but when it comes to more complex questions they, too, take a lot on faith. This is particularly obvious in those fields where experts strongly disagree, as in medicine, economics, or politics.

In a "hard" science like physics, objectivity is so strongly enforced that no disagreement among experts is allowed: if two physicists differ on a matter of physics, at least one of them must be wrong. Although most physicists will accept such a ruthless criterion for their science's objectivity, practicing researchers also know that this degree of stringency applies only to "finished physics" as it gets published, for example, in *The Physical Review*. But if one examines the thought process that leads to such a publication, the picture is quite different: in order for the researcher to make facts fall into an understandable pattern, he or she needs also to explore the surrounding territory that is not understood— that is, the researcher has to deal with faith. In this sense, it can be said that when Newton identified the force causing an apple to fall on his head with the one keeping the moon in orbit, he had to begin in the realm of faith; as did Einstein when he conjectured that a pulse of light moves at the same speed relative to all observers even if some of those observers are in motion relative to each other. Both were dealing with ideas that—according to notions current at their respective times—were, "objectively speaking," nonsense. True, the word "faith" may seem incongruous in this connection, perhaps because in common usage it is so often limited to a religious context; other words referring to the part of the universe that we don't objectively understand, such as "imagination" or "esthetic sense," are apt to be used instead. Yet Albert Einstein in particular apparently did recognize a quasireligious value in exploring the unknown; and many other scientists, who might not dream of associating their work with religion, will still acknowledge that such an exploration is strongly guided by an *imaginative* search for the *beautiful*—both of which qualities, according to our usage, are in the realm of faith.

When I was eight or ten or twelve I would have claimed that, because I am an utterly rational person, I take nothing on faith; faith, I would have said, is either for very young children or for not very intelligent adults. In fact, the claim that I take nothing on faith was patently false: since all children, including me, necessarily began their lives by taking *everything* on faith, it was quite impossible for the part of the universe that I did not understand to have shrunk to insignificance by the time I reached adolescence. Still, I hated to acknowledge that there was such a part. When some years earlier (as I recounted in a previous chapter) I drew a cross-sectional diagram of an airplane whose propeller was driven by a crank held in the pilot's hands, I could not possibly have believed that this was truly where a propeller obtained its power; but I preferred drawing something I understood—even if I knew it to be wrong—to putting into my diagram a blob labeled "MOTOR" about whose innards I hadn't the faintest idea. To have done so would have been an act of faith, which I apparently could not suffer.

I now believe that this total unwillingness to acknowledge the concept of the unknown, which for many years I blamed on the secularity of my upbringing, was actually something more personal, since I can now see that my father did not share it. Indeed, he was not known as a particularly tolerant man where his own values, that is, his own faith, was concerned; and his faith was in the mystical importance of the Yiddish language, for which he was willing to lay down his life—which in the end, in a sense, he did. In the context of the vibrant Jewish Vilna of the 1930s, and without prescience of the Holocaust, the aim of his work—to make Yiddish, and the institutions through which it could flourish, develop as a vehicle of modern twentieth-century scholarship so that it would command the respect of Jews and Gentiles alike—was generally seen as both praiseworthy and realistic, though some of his colleagues demurred at his singleminded and stubborn insistence that every detail be done absolutely "right" without cutting any corners. But when the Second World War destroyed that Jewish world and brought us as refugees to America, the external situation changed radically: not only did relatively few Jews here speak Yiddish, but those that did belonged almost exclusively to an older and uneducated generation that couldn't care less about "twentieth-century scholarship" and was in any case dying off. Yet my father's immediate reaction was that this was a change of quantity and not quality, requiring perhaps even more stubbornness, persistence, and willpower, but in the end America would come to support just as modern, educated, and creative a Yiddish-speaking culture as prewar Poland had been well on its way to doing. "Yiddish," my father was fond of saying, "will yet outwit history"—a statement of faith to rival any in the Nicene Creed.

Like most children, I originally accepted my father's faith on faith; in particular his idea of singleminded willpower, which (as I understood it) enables one to move mountains, appealed to me quite a bit. During my adolescence, I even went so far as to fast on the first day of every month "to train my willpower." My mother was not terribly happy but did not prevent me; as for my friends, they were somewhat bewildered (especially when they heard my explanation of the grand purpose of my fasting) but shrugged it off as one of Gabi's weird notions. But those notions came to a test when at the age of fourteen, attending summer camp in rural New York State, I one day at dinner announced that I could, entirely without help, drink the contents of the full one-gallon water pitcher that stood in the middle of the table; and in response to the skeptical noises of the other boys I put the pitcher to my lips. It was made of metal, and I clearly remember that, with my face closing off its aperture, it produced a deeply resonant and inviting sound. At last, I thought, the years of training my willpower would pay off in the admiration that I would earn for doing something that no one else could do. But after gulping down the first pint or so I sensed that this task was going to be harder than I thought; and having laboriously drunk what was probably the better part of a quart I put the pitcher down. I could not do it. I was defeated. In spite of what I thought of as my towering willpower, the mountain didn't move. It may, in fact, have been at that very moment that I lost faith in pure willpower—or, as I might put it in hindsight, I lost faith in faith. For the following few decades of my life I pretty much limited myself to physical science where, I felt, one deals only with objective concepts that are considerably less dangerous.

I certainly do not presume, on this basis, to pass judgment on my father, whose faith after all filled his life with enormous gratification but also on occasion with enormous pain (as genuine faith always does). But in my own mind Yiddish as a cause began to wane in importance. I do remember that a quarter of a century later, when Uriel died, my father poignantly implored me not to converse in English with Uriel's two young children, who up to that point had always been addressed in Yiddish in the immediate family. I looked deeply and lovingly into his eyes but did not reply.

In retrospect, it must be said that my previous faith in the unlimited efficacy of willpower had been, as the faith of children generally is, more primitive than that of adults in having only one origin: namely, what they hear from those whose authority they accept (most typically their parents). The faith of adults, on the other hand, can have four distinct sources, of which *hearsay* ("I have it on what appears to be good authority") is only one; in addition, there are *experience* ("I saw it with my own eyes"), *reason* ("It makes sense to me"), and *intuition* ("It's a hunch that compels my belief"). None of these four are, in themselves, objective, since authorities are sometimes wrong, our eyes all too often deceive us, things that appear to make sense can nonetheless be false, and hunches make no claim to objectivity at all. In some cases items of our faith can be made objective (and thus be removed from the realm of faith) by careful testing; yet it is out of the question to go through life applying such a scientific analysis to every single belief that we hold. Most of us don't have the qualifications to undertake such a serious research project in the first place, and it would in any case require far too much time and energy to keep up with all the perceptions with which life is continually flooding us.

But as far as *religious faith* is concerned, the situation is different because we know in advance that no valid objective arguments either for or against can be brought. Admittedly this last statement is itself part of my faith, and by no means universally accepted. Indeed, any number of books have been written purporting to present incontrovertible proofs of God's existence; while an approximately equal number of books take the opposite point of view. Nonetheless, I can objectively say that in all my years as an atheist I never encountered a convincing argument for the falsity of atheism; nor have I, in all my years as a believer, encountered the converse.

Religious faith has the same four sources—hearsay, experience, reason, and intuition—as faith of other kinds, but the conventional nomenclature is somewhat different: *Hearsay*, "I have it on what appears to be good authority," is now called *tradition*; and *intuition*, "It's a hunch that compels my belief," is now called *revelation*. The other two, *experience* and *reason*, retain their former names. Unfortunately, there has been a lot of misuse of these terms because of a lack of understanding that, to be valid, the four sources of faith have to refer to the believer himself. Thus tradition—"I have it on what appears to be good authority"—means "I have it on what appears *to me* to be good authority," not *to somebody else*; and revelation—"it's a hunch that compels my belief"—does not mean *someone else's* belief. Similar caveats apply to experience and reason. This is a crucial point because it shows that whatever one's faith is one must take real responsibility for it, a responsibility that it is logically impossible to abdicate. You cannot simply declare that you believe these things because somebody—your parents, your friends, or your church—tells you to, without reducing your whole faith to a childish one based on mere tradition (that is, hearsay); beyond that, *there is no way to will yourself into believing something that you don't believe.*

In Christian theology this represents a serious problem because faith, far from being an admission of weakness, is often presented as a sign of great power, as in Jesus's words: "O woman, great is your faith! Be it done for you as you desire"; or, on another occasion and to another set of listeners: "If you have faith as a grain of mustard seed, you will say to this mountain, 'Move from here to there', and it will move." Already in the letters of Saint Paul in the New Testament, and even more explicitly in later writers such as

Martin Luther, Christians are called upon to take whatever steps are required to strengthen their faith in order to earn God's reward and love; and Christian history is replete with stories of saints who subjected themselves to all sorts of privations hoping that by such a treatment their faith would be deepened. Unfortunately, such efforts often ended in disappointment (if not despair) because of the impossibility of attaining faith by one's own exertion.

Christianity's historical record in recognizing the logical impossibility of forced belief is not good. On the contrary, Christians have developed a special word—"heresy"—for failing to believe what one "ought to" believe; and a special punishment—burning at the stake—which for many centuries was the church's favorite sentence for heretics. In this connection it is interesting and important that the Greek word *hairesis*, from which "heresy" derives, means "choice," so that a heretic is simply one who *makes a choice* in what to believe, as indeed one is compelled to do by the sheer logic of faith.

True religious faith, rather than resulting from being told what one must believe, comes fundamentally from the definition of the word "faith"—"an acknowledgment of the part of the universe that we don't understand"—together with a notion that at the far edge of the part of the universe that we don't understand there exists a being that does understand it—for whom, in other words, *the whole universe is not only comprehensible but comprehended.* We refer to that being as "God." The four possible sources of faith—tradition, experience, reason, and revelation—are then seen as messages from God; in other words, the faith of the believer— as perceived by the believer—does not arise internally but comes as a gift from God.

The same logic applies to belief in miracles. I clearly recall an item the *Ann Arbor News* carried about fifteen years ago about a junior high school biology teacher who allegedly told her class that the virgin birth is a biological impossibility. Quite a fuss was raised over this, and (if I am right in my recollection) the father of one of the students even went so far as to bring suit against the Board of Education, claiming that his daughter's freedom of religion—meaning her freedom to believe in the virgin birth, which is what she was taught at home—was being attacked. "Well,

Gabi," one of my parishioners asked me at the time, "what do you think? Is the virgin birth a biological impossibility?" "Of course it is," I replied without hesitation, "otherwise it would not be a miracle." After all, the word "miracle" already signifies that the event in question violates the laws of science, but (as we discussed in an earlier chapter) the laws of science are not capable of ruling out an isolated unique occurrence. In other words, saying that it is a miracle does not preclude it having happened, and our Ann Arbor girl's freedom to believe in it is not affected in the least. Look at it this way: if God legislated the laws of science in the first place, there is no reason in the world why God cannot break them on a whim. But the real question, to a thinking person, is not whether God *can* but whether God *does*; why, in other words, would an omnipotent, omniscient God create laws of science that would later need to be broken?

Indeed, no such reason can be imagined unless *it is the breaking itself that is the point*, in the sense that by suspending the laws of science God is trying to tell us something. Thus the validity of a miracle, too, depends on *the perceived presence of an accompanying message*. Of course, perceiving the presence of a message does not necessarily imply a clear understanding of its content; the miracle of Jesus's resurrection, for example, has been acknowledged by Christians since the beginning of Christianity to carry a message of enormous significance, but opinions have differed markedly on what that significance might be. (Some Christians, in fact, will freely acknowledge that they are still searching.)

When I said that faith apparently does not arise internally in the believer but comes as a gift from God, perhaps "gift" was not the right word; perhaps "loan" would have been better. What I have in mind is that faith is not an attribute that, once acquired, necessarily remains constantly with us as though it defined the color of our eyes or the pattern of our voice. Indeed I know for a fact, having witnessed it both in myself and in my friends, that it is as impossible to have one's faith completely unassailed by doubt as it is to clap with one hand. For this reason, I tend to be somewhat skeptical both of believers who tell me that their faith never falters and of atheists who tell me that their atheism has never been assailed by momentary wafts of faith. This, too, has historically been a problem for Christianity, not only because of the common belief that faith is something one *ought to* have (so that one becomes a failure if one doesn't) but also because of the childlike and childish idea that one's faith has the power to legislate reality, so that not believing in God amounts to deicide. But of course the existence of God, if indeed God exists, does not depend on our beliefs; nor is God's love for us (in my opinion) any stronger if we do believe, nor weaker if we don't.

An immediate corollary of this understanding is that the validity of a miracle is an individual judgment, since you may perceive a message from God in an alleged event where I perceive no such thing. If the event is one that violates the laws of science it will then make sense for me to reject it as false, whereas you will probably embrace it as a miracle. Even for a single individual the perception of a message may waver with time: I, for example, for a long time flatly refused to accept the truth of the virgin birth simply because I could not figure out any message from God that I could attribute to it, but today I am not so sure. But then the condition of not ever being quite sure is, as we already said, a fundamental component of real faith.

In fact, part of the enormous admiration that I have maintained for my father all my life focuses on his ability to preserve the absolute integrity of his scholarship while doing research in areas that involved his faith and therefore must have called forth strong feelings of uncertainty. More than once I witnessed the profound pain he experienced when his science, represented by the unimpeachable honesty of his conclusions, collided with his faith, which sometimes made him wish that the conclusions had been different. My situation was, by my own choice, much easier: I had no emotional attachment to the atoms I was studying, and if my doctoral project called for measuring the hyperfine splitting of the metastable triplet state of helium-3 it made little emotional difference to me whether the result came out to be 6789.01 MHz or 6543.21 MHz as long as the number I reported was correct. Thus it was not true, as I pretended, that the reason I had no faith was that I had grown up in a family that had no faith: in fact, I had no faith because I was too frightened of it. Quite incidentally, my career choice of physics also pleased me as a demonstration of independence, since my father was as tone-deaf to physical science as he was to music. It would have been quite impossible for me to explain to him what "hyperfine splitting" meant, let alone why it was interesting to measure it.

Yet as I grew older, and as the experiences in my own life became more complex and began to involve other people in a more profound way (becoming a parent was an important example), I more and more began to feel that the part of the universe that could be logically comprehended was steadily becoming too small for me. Indeed science, which we defined at the beginning of the chapter as knowledge of the part of the universe that we understand, furnishes a great deal of comprehension but little room for choice; we can perhaps choose the topic of our research but certainly not what its results will be. There is no question, however, that making choices, especially in situations of great complexity, is one of the most fundamental of human urges and desires; and faith, being a simple acknowledgment of the part of the universe that we don't understand, provides us with an arena where there are many choices to be made, or in which (to use the Greek word) God's great gift of heresy can be freely exercised.

When I was five years old I refused to put into my cross-sectional diagram of an airplane a blob labeled "MOTOR" because it was too scary to acknowledge an entity whose innards I couldn't understand. Since today I have considerable familiarity with motors, that particular problem would no longer arise. On the other hand, the number of things in the world that I acknowledge *not* understanding, far from having decreased, has increased immeasurably; so that if I imagine drawing a cross-sectional diagram of the universe today, there would have to be quite a number of blank blobs in it. Their common label is "FAITH"; and although approaching them does on occasion waken some of the familiar anxiety, the gift of my older age is that, by and large, those blobs stand as proud and steady beacons helping me through a dark, uncharted world to places that I may not comprehend or recognize, but that feel surprisingly like home.

16 ❧ RESURRECTION

When still a child, I learned that a "religious festival" was a commemoration: Passover, for example, commemorates the Jewish exodus from Egyptian slavery. I also learned that it is typical for the stories of religious festivals to be embellished with supernatural features, like the magic acts performed by Moses in the palace of Pharaoh, or the parting of the Red Sea, but that modern people like us do not believe in those things. Only the realistic kernel of the story—in this case, that the Jews were once enslaved by the Egyptian kings but gained their freedom under Moses's leadership—constitutes the true historical origin of the festival.

I particularly remember learning about Hanukkah, another festival, early in elementary school. The teacher told us the rousing story of the Hasmonean uprising, the tale of an oppressed people (that's us, the Jews) under the harsh occupation of a Greek king named Antiochus Epiphanes, who desecrated the Jewish Temple in Jerusalem by bringing in his own idols (including one that represented himself) and forcing us to worship them. In 168 B.C.E., this triggered a popular revolt led by the priest Mattathias and his five sons known as the Maccabees, during which the occupying armies were expelled, the Jews regained their freedom, and worship in the Temple returned to its former glory. The class cheered. As an additional embellishment, we heard the story of the sealed cruet of lamp oil that was found in the Temple as it was being cleansed: it contained only enough undefiled oil for one night but, by a miracle, kept burning for eight nights. Religious people, the teacher explained, believe that this constitutes factual history; but even though we know better, it is still a charming legend, and Jews celebrate it every year by lighting candles in a Hanukkah menorah. The first night of the holiday we light one candle, the next night two, and so on until on the eighth night eight candles are burning.

On the other hand, as Jewish children in Vilna we did not pay a lot of attention to the various Christian festivals: for us the generic Yiddish word *khoge*, which means any occasion when non-Jewish stores are closed and churches busy, sufficed. In fact, it was probably not until I arrived in America and began to be exposed to the general gentile culture that I found out that Christmas commemorated the birth of Jesus Christ. Its story, too, turned out to be embellished with supernatural features, like the choir of angels seen by the shepherds, the arrival from the East of the three wise men to worship the baby Jesus, and of course the miracle of Jesus's mother Mary being a virgin (insofar as we understood what that meant). The general structures of the stories attached to Jewish and Christian festivals were, in other words, the same: a kernel of realistic narrative surrounded by miraculous events that, as far as I could see, no thinking person could take seriously.

There was, however, a single exception to this pattern, and that was the important *khoge* that fell around the time of Passover. Even as a child, I had noted that its Polish name, *Wielkanoc*, simply means "Great Night," revealing nothing of what it is about;

and many years later, when I was already a young adult in America and had many Christian friends, I still found it difficult to get a straight answer from them as to what exactly Easter commemorates.

I believe that my friends were shy in replying to an atheist like me because Easter is about an event that is pure miracle. It's not like Christmas or Hanukkah or Passover, where you can peel away the supernatural part of the story and be left with the historical, or at least the historically possible. After all, even atheists do not generally doubt that a man Jesus once existed, so there is no reason not to celebrate his birthday if one wishes; as to the shepherds' heavenly vision, or the three wise men guided by a star, or the claim that Jesus's mother Mary was a virgin—those details are no worse to an atheist than the legends of the Hanukkah cruet of oil, or the parting of the Red Sea, were for my parents and me. But the great miracle of Christ's resurrection, the miracle on which Christianity is founded, cannot hide behind otherwise realistic events, since if one omits this single detail there really remains no Easter story to tell.

The account itself is straightforward. It begins with the Passion, which is an old-fashioned word for "suffering." Jesus was crucified on a Friday on the eve of Passover (commemorated today as "Good Friday"). Some time late in the afternoon of that day the Roman soldier on guard, having verified that Jesus was already dead, allowed his friends to remove him from the cross and lay him in a temporary tomb. But the following Sunday morning (which is Easter Sunday), when a few of his female disciples came to embalm Jesus with the customary spices and prepare him for permanent burial (it could not be done earlier because of the Sabbath), they found that the huge boulder that closed off his grave had been rolled away and his body had disappeared. Later that day he showed himself fully alive to some of the disciples, so there was no longer any doubt among them that he had risen from the dead.

This was presumably the account that, under the title of *evangelion*—"good news"—spread like wildfire throughout the Greek-speaking Mediterranean communities, brought there (so I personally imagine it) by peculiar messengers, men with fiery black beards and fierier black eyes, who babbled in an incomprehensible Eastern tongue a strange report that, however, grabbed one by one's innards as nothing before ever had. Old men were found who could translate; their Aramaic was fragmentary, a few halting words and phrases remembered from their immigrant grandparents, now only used for ethnic in-jokes and occasional friendly obscenity. "They say that he is risen. They say that the messiah is risen. They say 'Alleluia, the messiah was crucified, and is risen.'" It would be another half century before the written Greek texts that we know as the Gospels, which tell the whole story in detail, began to appear. The old men were dead. The young men were old. The infants were grown. But the rallying cry of the "good news" that was setting the whole Mediterranean basin aflame continued to resound: "Alleluia, Christ is risen" ("Christ" being Greek for "messiah"); and in Christian churches at Eastertime it still resounds today.

But there had to be something more in the news brought by the bearded messengers, something to make the report of Christ's resurrection so immediately acceptable and meaningful to so many people. Since our earliest documents date from perhaps twenty years later, we can only speculate what it was. Most likely it was a promise that Christ, by his death and rising to life again, *overcame death itself* so that from now on those who were washed clean of sin would no longer be dying but literally live on forever; and that the way to wash oneself clean of sin was to undergo baptism—that is, to become a Christian. In a culture where only a small fraction of the population ever lived past middle age, nobody doubted that eternal life would be a consummation devoutly to be wished; furthermore, it made sense that such a reward would be limited to those who didn't sin and had taken steps for their past sins to be obliterated.

Obviously, however, the belief that everyone who undergoes baptism automatically becomes immortal could not survive the test of very much time; although one could explain away the first few Christians who died by hypothesizing that they sinned in secret after their baptism, to continue with such a theory would soon make a mockery of the whole idea. Accordingly, the perceived meaning of the resurrection was modified: those Christians who did appear to die were now believed to be transferred into a special state euphemistically described as "having fallen asleep"; but they would, it was assumed, come back to life at the moment of Christ's return, which was considered imminent. After that, they would live forever. This is the interpretation made by the oldest texts of the New Testament.

In time, however, that version also began to lose its force because of the delay in Christ's return. Even though the word "imminent" does not define a mathematically precise period of time, it does have a clear intuitive meaning; and if you have widely publicized the claim that all your friends and relatives who appear to have died will "imminently" rise to life again, there is only so long you can make your audience wait before they lose patience and start to call you crazy. And that is when another new theory appeared: Christians who die pass immediately into a blissful "life after death" in heaven, which then lasts forever; whereas sinners who die are, by contrast, condemned to an eternity of torment in hell. Opinions differed as to what exactly would happen when Christ ultimately did return to earth; but since that event was now relegated to a distant future, it would make little difference in most people's day-to-day planning.

I don't know to what extent Christians of the time realized how this last conjecture reshaped the very foundation of their belief. After all, had Christ's resurrection signified that baptized people would never die (as in the original interpretation) or die temporarily only to rise again a short time later (as in the "corrected" interpretation), the truth of that claim would become generally self-evident after a reasonable wait. But the new life-after-death theory must most definitely be taken on faith. It is quite likely, in fact, that this was the first time that the concept of faith took on the crucial role within Christianity that it has continued to occupy to this day.

When, as an atheist, I first encountered the Easter story I dismissed its literal content out of hand (since if the believability of a miracle indeed depends on the hearer perceiving in it a direct and personal message from God, then an atheist, who does not accept the existence of God, is precluded from ever believing in any miracle). And yet with time I began to feel that the story of Christ's resurrection did have an unusual profundity, though in what it lay I could not immediately discern. I did, however, definitely rule out the possibility that what validated the resurrection was the claim that it brought eternal life for Christians. Of course I have, then or now, no definitive information on the matter of life after death, nor does anyone else who has not died; I just did not, and still do not, feel that this is the message that the story of the resurrection brings to me. There are at least three reasons for this:

First, I reasoned that the whole idea of a "bottom line," a moment (presumably, the moment of death) when a balance is computed and a final decision made whether a person is "good" or "bad," is itself a human idea; God, if God exists at all, does not do that. If death is truly not the end of life, it also cannot be the end of human change or development, and so it cannot be an appropriate time for a final sentence to be pronounced. In fact, there can be *no* moment suitable for such a judgment.

Second, I found (and still find) the very concept of an "eternity of torment" to which sinners are supposed to be condemned decidedly repulsive; and God, if God exists at all, must surely find it repulsive as well. After all, a human parent would have to be psychopathic in the extreme to consign some of his or her children to a place of great suffering and throw away the key; surely God, the best of all possible parents (so I reason), could never behave like that.

Last but not least, the whole notion that baptism washes away human sins and so makes us more pleasing to God to the point where we are granted a place in heaven, while unbaptized people are condemned to spend eternity in hell, is one that I could not and still cannot accept. In my experience, people who are baptized are, on the average, neither morally better nor morally worse than those who are not; and insofar as God judges people at all, it must be done by looking into their hearts as much, or more, than into their baptismal certificates.

In fact I did, after a great deal of time and thought, identify the message from God that I feel the story of Christ's resurrection brings to me and that makes me believe in that particular miracle. I became conscious of it as I was reading a passage in the first letter of Saint Paul to the Christians of Corinth, in which he says: "We preach a *crucified Messiah*, a stumbling block to Jews and foolishness to gentiles." Clearly, the "stumbling block" and "foolishness" are not in the resurrection itself, which might have been considered plausible for a divine figure like Messiah (or Christ); rather, the mystery is: if Jesus was divine, then how crucified? and if not divine, then how resurrected? Thus neither the resurrection nor the crucifixion is all that significant by itself; it is only the two together that truly constitute the miracle of the Easter story—and they are, indeed, always recounted as one continuous narrative. In my opinion this Easter miracle remains, and was always meant to remain, a unique event, and eternal life (if it exists) has got nothing to do with it.

My idea, then, is that God, through the incarnation, was able to experience not only every kind of human joy but every kind of human suffering—even death on a cross. That is why the story of the Passion is always told so that the reader can most effectively identify with Jesus and recognize what he is going through. As for the question: How can God die? The answer is: Only if God is then resurrected! Yet Jesus obviously could not, at the moment of death, have had any idea that the day after tomorrow he would be alive again, otherwise his experience would have been radically different from that of any human being. No, the pain and agony, the terror and anger, the helplessness and despair, they were all as real for Jesus as they would be for you and for me; and so it remained until the very end, when after a final and desperate "My God, my God, why have you forsaken me?" he *really and truly died.*

That's why there was surely no one on that Easter morning two thousand years ago more surprised than Jesus himself: behind him the Passion, behind him the cross, behind him the final outcry; behind him the terror, behind him the knowledge that it finally isn't working, that it is finally too late. No, there was surely no one more surprised than Jesus himself as the white and gold splendor of morning light flooded past the rolled-away stone and he heard his own incredible cry: "Alleluia, I'm alive!"

But these are, of course, *my* thoughts. They need not be yours; they need not even be Saint Paul's, who also wrote various things contradictory to this point of view.

∞

The week that precedes Easter Sunday is called Holy Week; it begins with Palm Sunday (commemorating Jesus's triumphal entry into Jerusalem), and continues through Maundy Thursday (the day of the last supper), Good Friday (the day of the crucifixion), and Holy Saturday (the day during which Jesus presumably lay dead in his temporary grave). As it happens, on Wednesday of Holy Week in 2002 I had the first appointment with my neurosurgeon who, after inspecting the MRI films of my head that showed a brain tumor now the size of a tangerine, immediately began to plan the operation that would remove it. What with various required preparatory tests and procedures, however, the surgery itself was not scheduled to take place for another five weeks, providing me with ample time for recurring nightmares in which I was having my head cut open while totally powerless to resist. Curiously, although I attended church faithfully during that whole period, the parallel between my own immediate prospect and the prospect of crucifixion and resurrection never once occurred to me—even though descending into general anesthesia is about the closest experience to sudden death that I can imagine, and emerging again after some time has elapsed is exactly what being resurrected must feel like. But even though Gerane's reaction when I finally did return to consciousness was very much like Jesus's own: "Alleluia, Gabi is alive!" I myself was at that moment preoccupied with the difficulty I had in speaking—my vocabulary seemed to have shrunk to about three words—and the fact that the right side of my body was completely paralyzed.

As I write this it is Holy Week again a year later. My speech is almost normal except that I very often cannot recall a word on the tip of my tongue; and my right-side weakness is no longer obvious except for impaired balance and some lack of fine motor control. But these months of recovery, and especially the ap-

proach of Easter, gave me the opportunity to ponder what I
choose to see as Jesus's parallel experience, and to think about the
degree of his physical recovery. We do know—or at least the
Gospel of John tells us—that as Jesus hung, already lifeless, on the
cross, the Roman soldier on duty pierced his side with a spear;
and that a week after his resurrection Jesus himself invited the
apostle Thomas to place a hand in the place where the spear had
slashed him, and to feel with his fingers the holes left by the cru-
cifying nails. Apparently Jesus did not come through his ordeal
unscathed: crucifixion does leave its marks. Another Gospel reports that when, late on Easter Sunday, Jesus joined two of his disciples walking from Jerusalem to Emmaus, they failed to recognize him; and there are a lot of suggestions in all the Gospels that
the resurrected Christ seemed rather reserved and distant in dealing with his friends. Was he too, by any chance, slow in finding
his words? Did he too, perhaps, limp so badly that it was not till
he sat at the table in Emmaus and broke the bread that they suddenly realized who he was?

The old Jewish biblical legislation about the Passover em-
phasizes that the lamb for the paschal sacrifice (as also every
other animal used as an offering) must be "without blemish": it
would hardly do to offer as a sacrifice to God an animal that
would otherwise be classified as a reject and discarded anyway.
In drawing a parallel to the paschal lamb, some Christian writers
have insisted that Jesus, too, was "unblemished," but whatever
symbolic meaning that claim may have it cannot be taken literally. A human being with perforated hands and feet and a gash
in his side large enough for a hand to be inserted is certainly
blemished, blemished by the experience of crucifixion, blemished
in a manner that resurrection does not heal. This is true of every
one of us, and it is true of the crucified and risen Christ.

According to the Book of Acts (which is the most specific one
on this point), after his resurrection Jesus stayed forty days with
his friends before being taken up to heaven. I am thankful that
after my brain surgery I have already survived much longer than
that; and whereas I, too, will not last forever, I am already aware
of the degree to which I have been permanently changed. My

physical blemishes are such that I can never again climb a ladder, walk very fast, or preach formal sermons without a script in front of me; and walking up or down stairs is no longer possible unless I have one hand free to grasp a handrail. Yet at the same time my vision of the universe has become sharper and its colors more resonant; the people around me have become more interesting, more beautiful, and more challenging to understand; and the simple assertion that the sun will rise again tomorrow, far from being a triviality, has become an assurance of faith, of hope, and of love.

17 ❦ **GOD**

Even though my family was wholly secular and atheist, it was certainly never denied to me that there were other people in the world who did "believe in God"; I must therefore very early have had some inkling of what that statement meant. Indeed, if you suggest to a small child growing up in a reasonably functional household that "there exists an all-powerful and all-knowing being who cares passionately about you," the child will accept it readily: after all, isn't that what Daddy and Mommy are? What is there to believe or, for that matter, disbelieve? It's only when you begin to insist that the being in question is infinitely *more* all-powerful and all-knowing than Mommy or Daddy that a very small child becomes bewildered: one has to be somewhat older, or perhaps even much older, to grasp that concept. In my case, however, that was not a problem, since "we" did not believe in God.

Earlier in the book I recounted how, coming across the Yiddish translation of the Bible at the age of eight or so, I became fascinated by the creation account contained in its first chapters (which at that time was as far as I went). It was, to me, just a fairy tale, but a darn good one, to the point where I decided to embellish its narrative by composing my own version. There was no question in my mind, though, that the God of my story was my creation and not *vice versa*.

At the more mature age of thirteen, just after we moved to New York, I began to browse in the Yiddish Bible again. This time around my exploration covered a much wider range, and I remember being especially moved when I discovered the Twenty-Third Psalm ("The Lord is my shepherd, I shall not want"). The image of God as not only *a* shepherd but *my personal* shepherd, an intimate being at the same time powerful and gentle, felt intensely and warmly meaningful; and although I had no direct experience of having my head anointed with oil or a table prepared before me in the presence of my enemies, I found those metaphors enormously soothing. Without sharing with anyone what I was doing, I took to reciting this psalm silently every night as I was falling asleep, touching my hand to my forehead while doing it (in what feels to me now like a prefiguring of the sign of the cross), and intent on not allowing any extraneous thoughts to intervene or distract me from the intimate awareness of that personal shepherd. From time to time I discreetly repeated the same silent recitation and gesture when I was simply anxious about how something might turn out, as at the start of a school examination. It was, of course, a genuine prayer, deeply felt but also deeply lonely for being performed in secret.

The reason for my secrecy was, most likely, an uncertainty in how it would be received by my family. After all, I knew that "we were not religious," and at the age of thirteen I lacked the self-confidence to break away from that to a fragmentary "religion" that I had myself invented and that had no precedent in my former life. Yet it was that former life to which, I felt, I owed allegiance. America, where we had just recently arrived, was a totally alien world; and even though my family's odyssey could be viewed as having happily ended in the reunion of the four of us in New York, that other world to which I really belonged had, so it felt to me, been abandoned by us and was in mortal danger of being obliterated altogether (as indeed in the course of the following few years it was).

That is how, in addition to all the ordinary confusions of adolescence, I came to feel the need to make a decision as to which of two universes was truly real and which merely illusory: the universe of "back home," which in my childhood had always made such perfect sense that it seemed to be the one and only possible one; or the universe of America, which could not make that claim. The first universe was closed, meaning that anything outside it was by definition not very important; the second was wide open, which felt at some moments like a real breath of freedom but at others like the rupturing of a dike between me and a violent onrushing sea. And if the new universe included the rudimentary presence of God, who according to the old universe did not exist, that could hardly (I felt) be more of an illusion than pretending that we were still in Vilna.

Yet the path chosen by my father (as I perceived it), and therefore automatically by the rest of the family, was to insist on living in the first universe as though it were a bubble within the second. One example of this was that in our home on Payson Avenue Yiddish was the only language ever spoken. It's not that this rule was enforced by threat of punitive measures; it simply felt funny to use any other language. I don't think I ever held this against my father, knowing that for him the first universe was, in a sense, the only universe; but as time went on I personally began to feel uncomfortable living within that kind of constraint.

I have to admit that, in all of this, I had no awareness of God coming to my assistance; after all, I still consciously thought of myself as a committed atheist. But when much later, at the age of forty-five or so, I began to attend church regularly, I gradually came to the conclusion that I had been mistaken all those years: not "mistaken" in thinking that there was no God, but "mistaken" in thinking that I had ever been an atheist. The God of everything, I began to feel, was actually an old friend. The idea that this friend

lived "at the far end" of something, namely of "the part of the universe that we don't understand" (as I formulated it earlier), must
have crystallized in my mind during those first years in New York,
since my journey from Vilna had taken place across just such an
expanse, taking me from a place in whose multiplicity of languages I felt perfectly at home to one whose single language I did
not in the beginning understand at all. Indeed I have always, to
this day, visualized "the part of the universe we don't understand"
as a huge body of water, with God on a distant beach. Yet God, it
turned out, did live in America too, or at least visited regularly;
and somehow I sensed that this could help me out with the new
setting. "The Lord is my translator, I shall not want" was my very
comforting and frequent meditation, even though I always had
my tongue in my cheek when thinking it.

The search for a God who was the single God of everything
incidentally led me, as I was growing up, to the notion that one of
that God's most fundamental character traits had to be *tolerance*. In
fact, I realized almost immediately, divine tolerance must be rather
different from the human variety, which usually has its roots in not
really caring: it is very easy to be tolerant toward Christians, for example, if one doesn't have any strong feelings about religion to
begin with. The God I was seeking, however, must have the ability
to be deeply and personally invested in the truth of each of two
different points of view, both of which claim to be the superior if
not actually the only possible one, and to support them both
equally. Although human beings cannot easily fathom that, I believe that God nonetheless calls us to try; and I find that some
progress can often be made by constantly reminding oneself to pay
attention, not to the two points of view as abstract entities, but to
the real live persons who hold those opinions. God, I at length decided, is not much interested in abstract thinking; it may serve well
as an amusing distraction (as in physics or theology), but must not
ever be taken as important in itself. Above all, it is a serious error
to believe that it takes abstract thinking truly to understand God;
in my experience, it rather tends to confuse the issue.

The freedom that I now began to experience in thinking
about God reflects the paradoxical role that the concept played in

our Jewish society generally. In spite of our resolute atheism, we were still proud members of a historical culture that was profoundly steeped in the Jewish religion, so that modern Yiddish literature, for example, written mostly by atheists like us, nonetheless took God for granted as a part of everyday life. Thus I had implicitly been taught for many years that the Jewish God was the *real* God or, in other words, just plain "God"; whereas "their God," the Christian God, was just that—subsidiary almost to the point of nonexistence. I recounted earlier how, to my suggestion that "their God" was named Jezus Chrystus (as my little friend in Niemież had instructed me), my father replied that that was not exactly true: "Their God," he had said, "is, well, God." He could not quite say that "their God is the same as *our* God" since "we" didn't believe in God and so could not lay claim to one; but had he said that "their God is the same as *the Jewish* God," I would have found it very helpful. That he didn't was, I believe, less a matter of anti-Christian prejudice on his part than of the logical difficulty of equating two hypotheticals.

Is the Christian God really the same as the Jewish God? Yes and no. Classical Christian theology talks about "One God in three Persons," a concept known as the Holy Trinity, which certainly contradicts the Jewish absolute insistence on radical monotheism; yet Christians, too, claim that their belief is in one God and one God only. Fairly early in my church-going, I heard a sermon one Trinity Sunday, by a priest I knew and loved, that said something like this: "I freely admit that I don't understand the Trinity, but I also don't understand the theory of relativity. For me, it is sufficient to know that there are some people who do understand these things." I remember thinking then that such a point of view doesn't work for me because, as it happens, I do understand the theory of relativity quite well, having used it and taught it to students for a long time. As for the Trinity, I have had all sorts of ideas over the years in attempting to understand it; but as I became better versed in Christian theology I found that every one of my ideas was already well known, had a name, and was a heresy. I then realized that, unlike the case of relativity, *nobody* understands the Trinity; and that in fact the concept was, after a few early centuries of Christian wrangling, developed in such a way that nobody *could* understand it and therefore nobody could continue to argue about it.

Today I tend to think about the Trinity as really comprising two separate concepts: first, the rather abstract one that God is actually composed of more than one entity (specifically Father, Son, and Holy Spirit); second, that in addition to the Jewish idea of God (traditionally known as "God the Father" in Christian theology) Christians also worship a very concrete, personal, and intimate divine being called Jesus Christ, who does not correspond to anything in Jewish thinking. (Fairly soon after my ordination, I ran into an atheist Jewish friend who, totally puzzled by how I could possibly be at peace as an Episcopal priest, was nonetheless having difficulty articulating just where the source of his puzzlement lay. At last he found his voice: "Sooner or later, if you are a priest," he asked, "don't you find yourself having to pronounce the words 'Jesus Christ'?")

As far as the abstract more–than–one–entity idea is concerned, what it affirms to me is that whereas a child can be satisfied with merely exploring God as a *person*, intelligent adults have the further need to understand God as an *interconnection*. For example, the presence of God within the Trinity both as Father and as Son means that, just as we can say that each human being is created in the image of God, so is every parent–child relationship. This way of looking at it is important to me because it removes our tie to God from the excessively individualistic mode of thinking that generally characterizes our culture.

As for Jesus Christ, Christians have historically thought of him as "God the Son," theoretically the second person of the Trinity who, when incarnate in human form, became the Jewish itinerant preacher Jesus of Nazareth who was crucified by the Romans in the thirties of the first century and then, so Christians believe, raised to life again. In terms of "the far edge of the part of the universe that we don't understand," where God ordinarily resides, I visualize the incarnation as God tunneling under that part and emerging as Jesus Christ on our side, that is, inside the part of the universe that we do understand.

It would be not so much blasphemous as plain stupid for me to pretend that the purpose of God's doing this is known to me in more than a fragmentary way. That fragmentary way may, however, still be worth sharing. Above all, I absolutely do not accept any doctrine claiming that, at the time of the incarnation and crucifixion, the accumulation of human sin was so egregious that no ordinary punishment could ever sufficiently pay the resulting debt; only a death penalty executed with God as victim could constitute adequate atonement. This grotesque idea, which in one form or another has permeated much of Christian theology, can (as far as I can see) only be explained as itself a result of what in earlier chapters I called "cancer of the conscience" (which, as I also explained, is the meaning that I ascribe to the phrase "original sin").

Rather, as I understand it now, God's main purpose in producing the self-cloning that we call the incarnation was to have Jesus Christ, after an otherwise wonderfully fruitful ministry in Galilee and Judea, die an agonizing death on a cross in order to demonstrate to a very confused humanity that *suffering need not be a punishment for any sin,* and thus to free human beings from the cancer that has, since creation, afflicted their conscience.

Here is my understanding of how it was supposed to work.

"Many years ago," God mused, "I thought I could attack the problem by using my servant Job as an example. By choosing someone as clearly blameless as he, and subjecting him to a sequence of truly terrible experiences, I thought I would surely be able to demonstrate to my people that suffering does not necessarily mean punishment, because there is absolutely nothing that Job could possibly be being punished for. But did it work? No! Even his good friends, who loved him enough to set aside their own lives and come and sit with him in his misery, were unable to see the obvious truth. Instead, they got into speculations about Job's secret sins (of which, of course, there were none of any significance). The power of original sin was so overwhelming in the poor dears that they preferred inventing untruths about Job to admitting that there was simply no punishment involved. And when, losing patience, I tried to step in and explain the situation, they were so overpowered by the grandeur of seeing me at all that they didn't understand a word I said.

"But now I have a better idea.

"The problem with Job was that, being an ordinary mortal, he was, indeed, *capable* of sinning, which allowed others to speculate on what transgressions he might have committed that they simply did not know about. But suppose I send my own Son, himself an incarnation of me, as divine as I am. Obviously, God cannot sin, openly or otherwise! It is, by definition, impossible! And then, having established himself, he (that is, I) will be subjected to unspeakable pain and agony, ending with a terrible death. I myself will shoulder that burden; *I myself will be my own Job*. It will not, after all, be the first time that I suffer deeply for the sake of my beloved people.

"Of course there will be some who will say, 'That man was not really God.' Others will say, 'It was God all right, but God is incapable of such suffering, so the whole business must have been some sort of illusion.' Still, a few will surely get it, be inspired by it, and then, on the strength of their newfound freedom from the curse of original sin, explain it to the rest of the world."

Did it work? Almost, in that a sizable part of the world did come to accept Jesus Christ as God, and to acknowledge the pain and agony he underwent in being crucified. But when it came to understanding its significance, humanity balked. "He was God, and God is incapable of sinning," people said. "Therefore, the crucifixion cannot have been due to his sins, since there weren't any. Therefore . . . therefore . . . I got it! It must have been due to *my* sins! The crucifixion was *my* fault!"

At this, God wept bitterly, having lost once again. And so the work of salvation must continue into our own day and probably beyond.

But even if that specific purpose for the incarnation did not succeed, I believe that there were more general ones that did. First among them was to reemphasize the degree to which, in spite of clear omnipotence and omniscience, God still resembles human beings with regards to *feelings*. This explains what it means for creatures like us to have been "created in God's image" and thus to share, ever so imperfectly, in God's divinity. From that point of view, it may at first seem puzzling that the crucifixion has always found its focus not merely in feelings but more specifically in feelings of agony and pain, since it might easily be thought that to be all-powerful and all-knowing makes one able, by virtue of those qualities, to arrange to have everything happen as one desires and therefore not need to deal with suffering at all. But that is precisely the point: one of the central lessons of the crucifixion is that the greatest power does not, any more than the greatest weakness, affect the amount of pain that we feel. Pain is apparently something that nobody is exempt from, not even God.

Interestingly, Christians have always been aware of the agony of Jesus, to the point that in some circles the favorite form of a decorative or ceremonial cross is still the crucifix (which includes at the center a figure of Jesus hanging in helpless anguish); what's more, as we already pointed out, this awareness has often been misused to blame Jesus's suffering on our own sins and thus feed the guilt with which our cancerous conscience has saddled us. But the corresponding agony of all-powerful God the Father is often passed over all too lightly, even though it is perfectly obvious, if one thinks about it, that being (at least in the eyes of one's children; and in God's case, that's who we all are) omnipotent and omniscient really has nothing to do with it. The torture of being present when your child is nailed to a cross, and when in his agony he exclaims in a loud voice "My God, my God, why have you forsaken me?" is surely enough to make one wonder how even Almighty God can bear it. Yet asking who suffered more at the crucifixion—the Father or the Son—is meaningless, since it was in fact one pain, the same pain, that merged and enveloped them both. Indeed, I now appreciate that pain is, quite generally, not something that one can clutch to one's breast and say "This is mine": like Jesus' suffering on the cross or the Jews' suffering at the hands of their assorted persecutors, it must finally merge into a single pain that envelops everybody.

∞

Today, thirty years after I started going to church, my habit of doing so on Sunday morning (even if I am retired and no longer have any priestly duties) is more firmly established than ever. It is not however, nor was it ever, a matter of pleasing God; God, I am persuaded, would be perfectly content to continue to see me as an atheist, so long as my life remained constructive, creative, and loving toward my fellow human beings and the rest of the created world around me. What moves me to attend church today is that in the thirty years since I realized that I was not (and had in fact never been) an atheist I have become firmly addicted to praising and giving thanks to God, to the point that I would have real difficulty making do without it. Every Sunday in my pew, I rise at the first chords of the processional hymn and join with my friends, including those of other places and times, in what is primarily a service of thanksgiving. More specifically, we sing hymns; listen to some Bible passages and to a sermon that comments on them; join in intercessory prayers for the world, the church, and those whom we love; recite a general confession and hear the priest pronounce absolution; and finally unite ourselves with Jesus's original disciples in a celebration of Holy Communion. In all of this we give thanks to God, who is also our cherished friend, "for the splendor of the whole creation; for the beauty of this world; for the wonder of life; . . . for the mystery of love; . . . for the blessing of family and friends; and for the loving care which surrounds us on every side."

But the public church service, the kind to which the Episcopal prayer book refers when it calls itself the Book of *Common* Prayer, is not the only way in which my fellowship with God exhibits itself today. Admittedly, in spite of my having often explained to parishioners and friends that God may not always accede to our prayers but he absolutely always listens to them, I myself am still a bit shy when it comes to praying in private. Like a lot of other people, I tend to think that God, to whom my wants and needs are already known before I ever say them, has more important things to do. Yet every once in a while, especially at times of personal stress when I am anxious about how something might turn out, or more generally when extreme emotions like joy, fear, or grief threaten to overcome me, I do experience an overwhelming need to pray—not so much to tell God anything as simply to be in touch. It is at such moments that I find myself, likely as not, returning to the understanding I discovered long ago when I was still a thirteen-year-old boy who thought of himself as a committed and faithful atheist: concentrating first on not allowing any extraneous thoughts or images to intervene or distract me from the intimate awareness of that personal shepherd whom I now know to be God, I almost involuntarily touch my hand to my forehead and silently recite, in Yiddish, the text of the Twenty-Third Psalm.

CITATION INDEX